INVESTING IN F

Other How To Books on business and management

Be a Freelance Sales Agent
Buy & Run a Shop
Buy & Run a Small Hotel
Communicate at Work
Conduct Staff Appraisals
Conducting Interviews
Counsel People at Work
Doing Business Abroad
Do Your Own Advertising
Do Your Own PR
Employ & Manage Staff
Invest ing Stocks & Shares
Investing in People
Keep Business Accounts
Manage a Sales Team
Manage an Office
Manage Computers at Work
Manage People at Work
Managing Budgets & Cash Flows
Managing Meetings
Market Yourself
Master Book-Keeping
Master Public Speaking
Prepare a Business Plan
Publish a Book
Publish a Newsletter
Raise Business Finance
Sell Your Business
Start a Business from Home
Starting to Manage
Start Your Own Business
Taking on Staff
Understand Finance at Work
Use the Internet
Winning Presentations
Write a Report
Write Business Letters
Write & Sell Computer Software

Further titles in preparation

The How to Series now contains more than 150 titles in the following categories:

Business Basics
Family Reference
Jobs & Careers
Living & Working Abroad
Student Handbooks
Successful Writing

Please send for a free copy of the latest catalogue for full details (see back cover for address).

INVESTING IN PEOPLE

How to achieve higher standards and a competitive edge at work

Harley Turnbull

How To Books

Cartoons by Mike Flanagan

British Library Cataloguing in Publication Data
A catalogue record for this book is available from the British Library.

First published in 1996 by How To Books Ltd, Plymbridge House,
Estover Road, Plymouth PL6 7PZ, United Kingdom.
Tel: Plymouth (01752) 202301. Fax: (01752) 202331.

Note: The material contained in this book is set out in good faith for general guidance and no liability can be accepted for loss or expense incurred as a result of relying in particular circumstances on statements made in the book. The laws and regulations are complex and liable to change, and readers should check the current position with the relevant authorities before making personal arrangements.

Produced for How To Books by Deer Park Productions
Typeset by Concept Communications, Crayford, Kent.
Printed and bound by The Cromwell Press, Broughton Gifford, Melksham, Wiltshire.

Contents

List of Illustrations

IS THIS YOU?

Management trainee
Staff supervisor
Department head
Business student
Production manager
Sales manager
Job applicant
Accountant
Works/factory manager
Retailer
Business owner
Transport manager
Head teacher
Hospital manager
Catering manager
Partner
Director
College principal
Hotelier
Office manager
Voluntary work organiser
Customer services manager
Training officer
Project manager
Instructor
Construction manager
Youth organiser
Police officer
Fire officer
Prison governor
Social worker
Military leader
Section head
Community group leader
Mentor
Resort manager
Banker
Lawyer

Preface

The aim of Investors in People since its inception in the late eighties by the National Training Task Force and the Scottish Working Group has been to increase in the UK the levels of staff development and training. It has paralleled the dramatic increase in workplace-assessed qualifications, NVQs and SVQs.

Investors in People is a quality award which relates training and development to business goals. This book has been written to help those who have the task of steering organisations through the process. They could be staff members at all levels, consultants and advisers. Assessors, too, may be able to identify some useful points. Another interested group could be those who have heard about Investors in People and who want to learn more about it so as to decide whether they themselves should embark on a programme or simply to implement some of the strategies.

I am aware that there is already some excellent documentation on the 'Investors' process but in many separate pieces. Just as the development of an IIP process within an organisation should be seen as both a strategy and a system, so the logic of this may be more apparent in a single publication.

In the 1990s and beyond, well trained employees will be viewed as individuals with further potential and trainable talents who can be even more effective and organised within a work group or team. Quality is not just about effective production or service systems but also about people who have been efficiently selected, inducted, trained, developed and motivated. Training and development are therefore essential to business success.

To make the book as complete as possible, some short considerations of processes such as appraisals, inductions, business planning and employee surveys have been included. These are not meant to be exhaustive but to provide the reader with a pointer towards further reading.

I am indebted to Investors in People UK for permission to print details of the Standard and logo.

Harley Turnbull

In many parts of this book quotations from the Investors in People Standard are used within the text, especially in Chapters 3, 4, 5, 6, 7 and 8. Where these occur, the following statement applies to each one of them:

1
Introducing Investors in People

The title 'Investors in People' may well suggest to you a business programme which aims at the training and development of people – the UK workforce. To a large extent you would be correct. But Investors in People is more than that. It is part of a sea-change in the management of people and their development – harnessing education, training and human resources development (HRD) to a transformation of approach in the thousands of organisations, large and small, which together constitute the UK economy.

Investors in People is therefore a change programme for businesses of all sizes in which training and development are:

- related to business planning
- inspired by a vision of the future
- applied systematically in all sectors.

WINNING BUSINESS APPROVAL

Every organisation which has achieved IIP (Investors in People) is convinced that the whole process has been very worthwhile, probably essential.

Why? Important though it may be, it is not only because employees are better trained. It is because the business itself has been changed radically and for the better.

As W R Kerr, Secretary/General Manager of Malin Court, Ayrshire (a unique mixture of high quality hotel and excellence in the care of the elderly) wrote, 'Investors in People has given us a framework whereby the whole culture of our operation is continuously geared to developing and realising staff potential. I dread to think where we would be without the Investors in People experience.'

This is typical of the views of many successful businesses. For them Investors in People has resulted in:

- increased sales
- fewer complains
- higher quality products
- higher calibre job applicants
- preferential supplier status
- increased flexibility in meeting customers' needs
- new sources of sales and marketing.

It is not surprising, therefore, that by September 1995 the number of employees in Britain covered by Investors in People, either recognised or committed, was nearly a quarter of the total workforce, employed in over 25,000 organisations.

On the third anniversary of Investors in People (IIP) in November 1994, Mary Chapman, its Chief Executive, wrote in *People Management*, 'Companies who have already realised this [that their most important asset is people] include many household names who have achieved the standard – companies like Boots the Chemists, W H Smith, Unilever, ICI, Kwik-Fit, Land Rover, Yorkshire Bank and Vauxhall Motors. However,' she continued significantly, 'our biggest growth area for commitment is now small and medium sized companies. Over 34% of the recognised companies employ 220 plus people and over 40% employ 50 people or less.'

During Investors in People Week in 1995, organisations like Nationwide Building Society, British Steel and TNT were praising the effects of IIP.

> Alan Jones, managing director of TNT Express (UK) Ltd was reported in *The Times* as saying 'In ten years time, if you are not an Investor in People you won't be a serious player.' Tom Farmer, Chairman of Kwik-Fit, in *Financial Mail on Sunday* said IIP has helped boost profits by 58% in the last three years.

IIP applies to more than the biggest operators. Organisations with fewer than 10 people on their staff have achieved the Standard and, please note, the term 'companies' does not mean that IIP is restricted to the private sector. In fact, there has been much interest in the public sector – police, education and schools, Benefits Agency, and River Boards. In 1995 some 200 schools and colleges had already been recognised and nearly 2,000 were committed to its achievement.

Targets

Are there **national targets** for achieving Investors in People? The answer is yes.

The National Advisory Council for Education and Training Targets aims for the targets by the year 2000:

- Seventy per cent of all organisations employing 200 or more employees, and 35 per cent of those employing 50 or more, to be recognised as Investors in People.

- In Scotland, 70 per cent of all organisations employing 200 or more employees, 35 per cent of those employing 50 or more, and 15 per cent of those employing under 50, to be recognised as Investors in People.

As you read this perhaps you are asking yourself if your organisation should be part of these targets. The rest of the book should help you make a positive decision.

INCREASING STAFF MOTIVATION

The process of reaching IIP status involves change in many organisations, change on the part of both employees and management. Much of this may be attitudinal:

- Senior managers have to learn that the training and development of employees is a source of success and profit rather than extra expense leading to no apparent benefit.

- Staff have to see that **their** contribution is vital to the organisation's success, in partnership with management.

A determination by management to identify each employee's role in realising their business objectives leads to the highly motivational feeling of involvement in the company's success by both manager and employee. When senior management convey to line managers and supervisors their role in achieving Investors in People, they are not just communicating, they are **motivating** them by recognising their importance. In the same way, supervisors motivate their staff by showing individual interest in the training and development of their teams.

Communicating with the workforce

Investors in People is a **people-centred** approach, enlisting the skills of the workforce in striving for success. To be really effective it demands excellent communication within an organisation through:

- publicising the intention to commit to IIP
- listing its advantages for both individual and company
- relating all training to the business plan and company vision
- familiarising each employee with the plan and his/her role
- reporting on progress
- holding regular meetings on training and development.

INVOLVING THE WHOLE ORGANISATION

Some psychologists base their strategies of motivation on people striving to meet their individual needs. For example, Maslow, in his well-known hierarchy of needs, suggested that those at the base of the hierarchy are physiological and safety needs. Further up the scale are psychological needs for the feeling of belonging, for love, affection and esteem and self-actualisation (reaching one's full potential). David McClelland emphasised the need for achievement, balanced by the fear of failure. Provided there is not too strong a chance of failure, the need for achievement can be extremely motivating.

Undoubtedly motives such as self-actualisation and achievement will motivate individual managers and staff to participate enthusiastically in an IIP programme, but involving the whole organisation is best done initially through such group influences as:

- participation and empowerment (responsibility)
- relevant training and development directed towards company success

- justified faith and trust in the organisation by employees
- good two-way communication
- pride in being part of a successful, progressive organisation.

Nearly always, organisations that aim for Investors in People are **ambitious**, **go-ahead** and **efficient**. They are confident they can, sooner or later, reach the Standard, without being over-confident. Of course individuals who form part of IIP Project Teams do look for self-recognition as well as team recognition (see later section on Motivation). IIP, in fact, emphasises training, development and evaluation at individual, team and organisational levels. So it undoubtedly motivates, through co-operative effort and individual ambitions.

STARTING AN INVESTORS IN PEOPLE PROGRAMME

If you are really interested in Investing in People and you would like to make a start in your organisation you should:

- complete reading this book – and keep it for future reference
- contact your Training and Enterprise Company, TEC (in Scotland LEC), who will advise you on specific help they can provide.

At the same time, you should try to obtain a **general understanding** of the Investors in People Standard. Scan over the four principles and 24 indicators (page 169). At first covering all of these requirements may appear to be a lengthy and difficult task. However, as you familiarise yourself with the indicators, you will gradually see they form part of a philosophy of business which emphasises the role of people. If you are broadly in agreement with this philosophy, your own positive attitudes will go a long way towards helping you to reach your target.

Assessing your own attitudes

If you are still in doubt, consider each of the following questions and ask yourself if you can honestly say 'yes'.

- Do you believe in the importance of staff training and development?
- Do you think that training should relate to your business plan?

- Do you believe in ever-improving communication within your organisation and with your customers?
- Are you willing to provide a training budget and staff time to achieve Investors in People?
- Do you favour induction and appraisal systems which emphasise employees' training needs?
- Are you in favour of checking the effects of staff training on reaching your business aims?
- Would you continue to be committed to investing in people in future?

Do you generally agree? When you take each of these ideas and ask yourself if you are already putting them into practice or how you will (if you do not already do so), you will begin to like the process of building a new and more effective system of people development.

Where you should start

Using the booklet, The Investors in People Standard, IIP, UK 1995, or the Diagnostic Pack, Scotland 1993, IIP, sit down with several colleagues and, together, work out how your organisation stands in relation to the 24 assessment indicators (see further details in Chapter 3).

As an example, take one particular indicator from the Diagnostic Pack:

> *2.3 A process exists for regularly reviewing the training and development needs of all employees.*

This is self-assessed by asking yourselves five questions and answering Yes (10 pts), Partly true (5 pts) or No (0 pts).

In considering how you might reply, we will assume that you already have a pilot appraisal interview system for some staff at all levels and a training programme for those managers who are conducting the interviews. The appraisals deal with the training required in relation to the organisation's business plan. The figures in brackets are the answers you are, notionally, giving.

	Yes	*Partly true*	*No*
Are individuals' training needs identified?	10	(5)	0

Are the people who carry out the reviews competent to do so?	(10)	50	0
Are the reviews carried out regularly?	10	(5)	0
Are individuals' needs identified in the context of business objectives?	(10)	5	0
Does the process cover all employees?	10	5	(0)

Total – 30: Maximum – 50: Percentage – 60

The result shows that for this indicator some processes are still required, *eg* applying the system to all employees permanently would be priority one for the working group. As the system is, for the time being, a pilot only, there has not been time for it to be carried out regularly but it has the potential.

You should also make sure that such a process is actually functioning and bedded-in before your assessment for IIP recognition.

Answer all the questions to find out from the full audit exactly how your company is placed at the moment in relation to requirements. Then start your action plan (see page 45). If there is disagreement as to whether you should score 10 or 5 or 5 or 0, tend to decide on the lower rating and work to reach the highest rating. A similar diagnosis can be achieved by looking at the Investors in People Standard booklet, page 24, and studying the Guidance and Key Questions sections.

MASTERING THE PRINCIPLES

Earlier in this chapter you were steered towards making a preliminary scan of the Investors in People Standards. We shall now set about this overview thoroughly.

In 1988 the National Training Task Force started to plan the IIP quality standard. They rapidly produced a set of ground rules compiled from the views of successful business people. These **principles** and **assessment indicators** are ingenious in conception and highly effective when implemented. The idea of detailed indicators stemming from the four principles reflects a logical system which works in practice.

Even the title is exceptionally appropriate. Take the word 'invest'. According to the *Penguin English Dictionary* it means 'to lay out (money) in order to obtain returns on it'.

The *Collins Concise Dictionary* says 'to endow with qualities, attributes, etc, to spend time, effort, etc, with the expectation of some satisfaction'.

Both of these meanings reflect the way in which properly planned and directed training produces dividends. It does 'obtain returns' and it does 'endow with qualities'.

For your company/organisation to achieve IIP standards, you must show that your people management policy is governed by the four principles.

Principle = fundamental truth or element, or more simply, a RULE

We consider each of these four now and consider fully what they mean. All of the rest of your endeavours will fall into place if you keep these in mind.

1. Commitment

An Investor in People makes a public commitment from the top to develop all employees to achieve business objectives.

Key phrases		*Meaning*
From the top	–	board of directors, chief executive
Public commitment	–	a promise to the whole workforce of the organisation
All employees	–	means 'all', from managers to cleaners
Business objectives	–	the aims of the business plan

2. Planning/Review

An Investor in People regularly reviews the needs and plans the training and development needs of all employees.

Key phrases		*Meaning*
Regularly reviews	–	at specific times, or every six or twelve months, employees' training needs are actively considered.
Plans the training and development needs	–	the supervisor or line manager agrees with the employee a programme of objectives for training relevant to the individual's development and the organisation's training strategy to achieve the aims of the Business Plan.

3. Action

An Investor in People takes action to train and develop individuals on recruitment and throughout their employment.

Key phrases		*Meaning*
Takes action	–	provides effective training in the workplace or on a course.
On recruitment	–	during the induction process
Throughout their employment	–	at all times, no matter what age or stage, all staff must be constantly updated.

4. Evaluation

An Investor in People evaluates the investment in training and development to assess achievement and improve future effectiveness.

Key phrases		*Meaning*
Evaluates the investment	–	ascertains the effects of the cost/effort put into training, its worthwhileness in terms of increased turnover, profit and quality.
To assess achievement	–	to quantify improvement, *ie* in terms of quantity, or the reaching of precise objectives/targets.
To improve future	–	to apply findings to future training policy effectiveness on product and service development.

Evaluating the effects of Investors in People really involves two groups of three elements, *ie* you should take into account the process of training and development:

(a) before, (b) during, (c) after training

and its effects on:

(a) individual, (b) group, (c) organisation.

SUMMARY

In this chapter the following points have been made:

- IIP has won the respect of UK businesses and public organisations.
- By employee participation in achieving IIP, motivation and morale are increased.

- Starting an IIP programme involves the identification of key training and development processes which require to be put in place or improved.

- Understanding the principles of IIP is vital in the successful planning of a programme to achieve the Standard.

Now assess your own attitudes and thoughts by thinking about, discussing or debating with your colleagues the Case Studies and Discussion Points.

CASE STUDIES

Ken Hill, inner city project manager

Ken Hill, age 40, is the Project Manager of an Inner City Urban Regeneration Scheme, funded by the local authority, central government, the local TEC and a consortium of local businesses. Ken is adept at obtaining funds from other sources as well as co-ordinating the efforts of his diverse management board.

To obtain the Investors in People award, Ken thinks, would help ensure their continued support and that of other potential funding agencies. He has a core staff of 20 who negotiate and arrange various initiatives such as housing co-operatives, and small business and entrepreneurial ventures by local people.

In managing his internal staff, Ken is much less successful than with his sponsors. He finds it difficult to make decisions, set targets for individuals, carry out effective costing procedures or to plan ahead in detail. Priding himself on his 'democratic' approach he leaves all decisions to the whole 'team'. He sees his role as an overall supremo, not bogged down with unnecessary details. When in the office, he is always on the phone about some new, exciting project. His desk is totally clear. In his favour, he is keen on virtually every kind of training for staff, even if it is not always relevant.

When the staff voted by 16 votes to 5 in support of doing Investors in People, only Nora Thomson, Office Supervisor, and her group voted against.

Alex Thompson-Bell seeks a badge of distinction

Alex Thompson-Bell, age 36, was recently voted local businesswoman of the year in the relatively prosperous Midlands town where, seven years ago, she set up her own upmarket Interior Design company. Even during the Recession her business has flourished because of her creative flair and determination. Clients from all over the UK vie for her services. The AT-B designed interior is a real status symbol.

In addition to her Personal Assistant, Ruth Trotter, she employs nine other staff, including two males. She thinks that if she obtained Investors in People as well as the recently achieved ISO9000, it would be a further badge of distinction, as well as good publicity in the local and national press.

No one denies that Alex is very hard working. She is also very conscious that it is her business, owned and run by her and no one else. Although claiming that her weekly staff meetings are 'group discussions', she is extremely autocratic, deciding on every detail without any discussion at all. As part of the process of working towards IIP, she is considering telling staff that they will all start on an MBA course.

Vernon Watkins coasts towards retirement

Vernon Watkins, 57, is in charge of Human Resource Development (formerly 'Personnel') at PACTEC PLC, packaging manufacturers for a variety of industries, including Information Technology. There are 537 employees. Vernon is very efficient in all the conventional aspects of the job and is people-centred as opposed to production-centred. He has been with the company since its early beginnings some 30 years ago. In his time, he was regarded as a high flyer in Personnel circles, renowned for his belief that 'a happy workforce is an efficient workforce'.

For a long time now, however, he has been content to rest on his laurels though still demanding a very high standard in routine activities from his two assistants. He is really now coasting along towards retirement in two or three years, in contrast to the dynamic energy of his livewire senior assistant, Ryan Hunt, who has been pestering Vernon to computerise all the HRD records and programmes. Ryan is keen on the hard-headed technological approach to management, soft pedalling on what he regards as woolly, soft 'ploys' (as he calls them) such as employee 'empowerment'. He goes along with these ideas, however, so as not to appear negative to senior management.

Ryan impresses the executive director

'What will they think of next?' Vernon Watkins asked himself as he walked contemplatively away from the monthly meeting of managers at PACTEC PLC.

'I suppose you'll be going for it', observed his 25 year old assistant, Ryan Hunt. 'I think we could make a real impact on this organisation the way we handle this – it'll give us all sorts of possibilities for pushing the department forward – involving us in more business decisions.'

Vernon wasn't so sure. He had been interested, even pleased, to be an obscure member of the BS5750 (now ISO9000) committee, but now

James Goodlad, the executive director, after some explanatory talks with the local TEC, wanted PACTEC to achieve the Investors in People award. It would mean looking at all the details – in his hand was the sheet with lists of 'Assessment Indicators' underneath each of four principles – restructuring the role of HRD, probably even changing its whole policy.

'I'll play for time and hope it blows over,' Vernon planned.

And so he did, politely dealing with memos about Investors, being cooperative with the TEC, but pleading overwork and other holdups for long delays in arranging meetings or replying to enquiries.

Thus three months went by, with little happening.

One day, James Goodlad called him in. Far from being critical, impatient or annoyed, he greeted Vernon with delight.

'I really must congratulate you,' he smiled, 'you really have enthused young Hunt.'

'That summary he handed in to me of your department's diagnosis of where our organisation stands at the moment in relation to achieving IIP and the draft Action Plan are really excellent – Please keep up the good work.'

'Oh, by the way, the extra points he made also about the advantages for us and its impact on our customers are really worth using in future.'

Vernon was literally stunned. What on earth was he going to do?

Should he give Ryan a real telling off for brazen underhand interference?

Give him enough rope to hang himself?

Or could Ryan be right?

Question

Sometimes longer serving managers are thought to lack flexibility, sometimes called 'hardening of the categories'. But this is often an unfounded belief held by younger colleagues and sometimes by themselves. Do you think that older managers (and their employers) should be more confident of their abilities to lead new projects and, indeed, to achieve new qualifications?

DISCUSSION POINTS

1. Have you always related staff training to a Business Plan? If not, do you agree that it really makes good business sense?

2. Some managers and employees may initially lack enthusiasm for Investors in People. Why should this be when they can only gain from it?

2
Preparing for Change

You have now completed your initial audit of your organisation's present state of progress towards the Investors in People Standard. Whatever your findings, whether you think it will be easy or difficult, you now have to take action.

MAKING CHANGE HAPPEN

Where do you start? By communicating with everybody.

The key word in organisational change is COMMUNICATION

The head of your organisation must convey the decision to proceed towards IIP to all staff. And everyone must know what IIP is all about.

How do you do this?

1. A brief note explaining IIP is sent to every individual member of staff – see Figure 1.

2. Top management and team leaders explain the details.

3. Details of:

   - the **principles** and **indicators**
   - the organisation's **mission statement**
   - the **business plan**
   - types of **training** that will be required
   - the **development/appraisal interviews**

   will be circulated at the team leaders' meetings. These papers must not be long and complicated. You must issue the IIP Standards

To all colleagues
What is Investors in People?

Investors in People (IIP) is a national standard about your training and development.

The company, to achieve this recognition, must have a business plan.

We will, as part of our programme to reach IIP Standard:

1. Provide you with this necessary training and development for you to meet our customers' needs.

2. Identify your training needs during induction and regularly afterwards.

3. Interview you annually so as to discuss your training needs.

4. Inform you of the company's business plan and your role in it. Issue you with the Action Plan for achieving IIP.

5. Seek your co-operation in deciding whether your training has been effective, relevant and worthwhile.

You will be given more details during large, whole staff, meetings, at your departmental/section meetings and in the company's newsletter.

We believe that the successful achievement of IIP will lead to more business for the company, increased profits, and more employment.

Fig. 1. Explaining IIP to all staff.

as they are, but the rest can be summarised and clarified. The Mission Statement should be displayed prominently at various parts of the workplace, including the main entrance. It is really important that no employees will be able to complain, 'No one told me about it'.

Remember that in all written communications you should:

- keep vocabulary as basic as possible
- use short sentences
- be concrete (not abstract).

If possible, everybody should also be given a note of the training they have received through the organisation over the last two or three years. If training records have not been kept, a system should be started.

Sometimes staff forget about training or have not recognised some activities as being part of a training process. If they have their own copies of such training, they could talk about it with more confidence.

Remember also that training should not appear to be forced on people. If this happens the workforce can become suspicious or resentful. Training and assessments for Vocational Qualifications (S/VQs) can lead to responses such as: 'Are you suggesting I can't do my job after 20 years' experience?'

This kind of reaction shows lack of preparation and communication. If these two factors are adequate then most people will be co-operative – indeed re-motivated by the fact that someone is taking a real interest in them as individuals. This may mean a change in organisational culture.

Importance of culture

Culture is about the shared image all the people in an organisation have about the way things happen or are done. Sometimes these ideas are positive and helpful – 'we believe in good quality and excellent service' – and contribute to keeping things going.

If change involves a real culture change, however, it can prove difficult to bring about. If a company has staff who specialise in training, it will be more difficult to persuade team leaders that their job is more than a supervisor's and that it also involves training and mentoring.

Other changes could be:

- new staff selection methods

- new qualifications
- new ways of measuring production.

All of these could happen in the process of achieving Investors in People. Explaining and communicating are both required but you, as an organiser, may also have to persuade and negotiate.

PERSUADING AND NEGOTIATING

No matter who you are – director, manager or employee – if you are enthusiastic about an IIP programme you can expect to have to meet and overcome objections from your colleagues.

Why should this be?

In every project which involves change there are **positive** motives of achievement and ambition and **negative** equivalents of fear and anxiety.

The following are examples of these often perfectly genuine attitudes and how, by persuading and negotiating, you can hope to bring about a more positive approach.

Fear of new roles and responsibilities

Line managers and team leaders may worry about their roles in staff development, *eg* interviewing/appraising staff, chairing meetings to discuss group training or instructing people themselves.

If they are assured they will be given training and practice in the new processes and can see this is done they will often become enthusiastic about this new role. Such skills can be learned, especially the abilities to identify problems, to listen and to discuss possible solutions.

Attacking the policy – it's a waste of money and resources

Directors or senior managers may not really believe in the importance of training and development – or indeed of a well motivated workforce who are proud to work for the organisation. You can point out to them that training costs do not need to be as high as they say – a good deal of training can be done internally by staff members. 'All right', they will say, 'what about the time involved as well as the fee for IIP assessment?'

Remind them of the gains for successful organisations which have been proven time and again and far outweigh the cost in money and time needed to achieve them. Even more important are the unquantifiable gains in terms of organisational morale and positive attitudes.

Our employees don't need or want training and qualifications. If they do *achieve extra qualifications, they will leave anyway. Other companies will gain from our expense.*
You can point out that training is nearly always needed for new and existing staff often because of developments in technology. If staff are deprived of training, lack of competence will lead to stress, lower production and poorer quality. What's more, the evidence is that well trained staff are much less likely to leave than those whose needs have been neglected. To assume nowadays that most staff are unambitious and just want to make money, with no job satisfaction, is a mistake.

Our Personnel/HRD Department will feel that their role is being undermined if line managers are involved in appraisal interviewing and employee development.
This is an unlikely difficulty since HRD has a major co-ordinating part in any Investors in People programme and they will also be involved in training line managers for their role. They will also have considerable responsibility in the evaluation of the whole IIP process. This means devising precise ways of defining production or service targets, setting objectives for the various groups, measuring effectiveness and providing feedback.

We do nearly everything already that is required by IIP – in fact our employees are entitled to a generous amount of time for training. So why bother with IIP?
Because with IIP there are several new processes which you may not already have linked to training and development, *eg* directing the training of individuals and groups specifically towards business objectives and then evaluating the effects of training. Even changes like these involve a change in culture. Training in itself and without a clear objective may well be a waste of time.

If we are given more training, more work may be expected of us for no more pay.
The majority of staff will want to improve their qualifications so as to be in line for promotion to better paid jobs. The whole IIP climate should change the 'them and us' culture.

'Winning' the argument

Whoever said 'you never **win** an argument' was highly perceptive. Even if you do score more plus points in a logical discussion, your opponent will be resentful and find it difficult to co-operate in any programme.

Therefore the way you harness the various points made above will make all the difference to the actual processes for achieving IIP.

In any argument, there are one of three possible outcomes:

- win/lose
- lose/lose
- win/win.

In the first of these, a senior member of staff may simply order a subordinate to follow a course of action. The loser will obey, but not positively or well. In the lose/lose situation, an intractable conflict may be settled by arbitration where a solution is imposed which neither party likes or wants. Best of all is the win/win solution where:

- both persons/groups agree on a common aim (to see the organisation prosper)
- both sides are willing to give and take – negotiate
- discussion takes place with a determination to settle the argument
- time is allowed to reach an agreed position
- both achieve a measure of 'success'.

INVOLVING EVERYONE

It is really important that everyone from the chief executive to the most junior employee is aware of and involved in the IIP project.

This means:

- excellent **communication**
- **openness** about every aspect.

If not, rumours and alarmist speculation often result from:

- closed discussion amongst management
- isolated pieces of information filtering out
- feelings of powerlessness resulting from non-involvement

- annoyance about lack of information.

Very few organisations deliberately keep their staff totally unaware. They may publicise the fact that they are committed to the principles of IIP and tell employees about their intentions – but wait till the last minute to inform staff properly.

What is needed is the type of information described earlier in this chapter.

If every employee can see that **their** training relates to the business plan, then their commitment to IIP and the organisation will increase. Working towards qualifications such as S/NVQs and taking part in external courses which relate to their present jobs or possible future jobs will clearly be relevant to the workforce.

However, it is important that training and development are seen as belonging to a wide range of activities:

- longer courses at a training location at a distance from work
- training sessions at a training centre at the workplace
- frequent group training from the line managers/team leaders at work
- short individual, monitoring session with a team leader.

Sometimes the last two of these may not be perceived as 'training', so it is important that all such experiences are recorded in an individual training record, and that the employee is made aware of how each of the sessions is contributing to the aims agreed during an appraisal interview. Therefore the objectives of all training should be clarified at the start so that their achievement can be part of the evaluation process.

Progress toward systems which are generally regarded as of real importance to an IIP organisation, such as appraisals and inductions, should be reported in newsletters/newssheets, *eg* 'All new members of the staff go through an induction process which consists of . . . . If you have a change of job within the company, then you will be inducted into your new role.' Programmes as examples of these inductions could be described.

Such processes are not only relevant to IIP, they are good for the organisation as a whole.

The role of the consultant

Just as all full or part-time members of an organisation should be actively involved in IIP so should an **external consultant**. It is important to know how to make efficient use of the consultant's expertise. He/she can:

- discuss with senior management the Standard and the processes
- help construct and write up a business plan and the associated training and development
- give talks to large and small groups on aspects of IIP – the portfolio, the assessment process
- help you construct an IIP action plan
- advise you in setting objectives and evaluating the related training.

The consultant should be given the opportunity to get to know your organisation and its staff really well. This means that he/she will have access to the business plan (if there is one), be able to talk to and advise individuals and groups in their roles and carry out a trial assessment if you wish to have preliminary practice. He/she should become essentially one of the staff, being known to everyone personally.

Focus groups

One important involvement factor is for one or, better, several staff members to attend regularly meetings of your local focus group – meetings organised by TEC or LEC where organisations committed to or having achieved IIP attend sessions where talks/discussions/exercises are provided to help companies achieve or re-achieve Investors in People – simply exchanging views and experiences can be a most helpful part of the learning process. You also become aware of the great variety of organisations involved locally – large and small, production or service, public or private sector. The fact that IIP is so adaptable to all of the groups shows its essential strength and universality.

MOTIVATING PEOPLE

So enthusiasm about investing in people can be accelerated in your organisation by people involvement. But such processes mainly relate to **group** behaviour.

To influence most people really effectively, however, we have to think about the factors which activate them **individually**.

Two forms of motivations have been identified:

1. External factors (exogenous)
2. Internal human 'mediating' factors (endogenous)

External factors
External incentives can be linked to internal needs.

Need	Incentive
Security Achievement Self-esteem	Money Promotion Recognition

Example: a manager may take up and lead an IIP programme so that, if successful, he may receive a higher salary, a better car and/or promotion. He/she may also do it to fend off anxieties such as fear of failure. If generally successful, his/her behaviour will be reinforced, *ie* all the effort, work he/she has done will be continued and maintained so as to retain the positive rewards. The main point is that rewards – even the very effective word of praise – should be continued, but not so often as to become not worth having. If the culture of the company is based on the status of 'climbing the ladder' then this kind of motivation will be very effective, especially if the manager's subordinates are all rewarded in the same way for their efforts. Even in a more democratic, flatter structure, the team will respond to praise and group incentives, *eg* equal bonuses all round.

Internal factors
But the other 'endogenous' theories warn us of the potential limitations of such techniques. If the manager has made great efforts and has been successful in steering the organisation to achieve IIP but his/her rewards are not equivalent to his/her expectations, then de-motivation will occur. So it is important to define what kind of recognition will be given for success – even if it is essentially 'recognition' rather than the more tangible, concrete type of reward.

For most employees, the motivation lies in the effects of the new procedures themselves and group success. Having one's skills updated makes you yourself a more commercial product. 'What matters now', according to Waterman and Waterman, 'is having the competitive skills required to find work when we need it.' Loyalty, therefore, is to one's own career rather than to a potential employer. 'The employer and the employee share responsibility for maintaining – even enhancing the individual's employability.' Of course, the employee will want to stay with a good employer, but if this is not possible, he/she has these relevant skills. In the 'learning organisation' – one which takes active steps in creating new strategies to be successful and where there is constant communication – training and development give it the competitive edge and the individual employee is career resilient. Hence IIP is good for both individual and organisation.

Staff interaction

Employees of the organisation must also **interact** and discuss IIP and the new training and development procedures with each other. This can be organised in various ways with a range of groups:

- all employees (small organisation)
- divisions (medium organisation)
- department (large organisation).

With groups of this size, the main purpose would be:

- to provide a report on progress
- to have a talk on, for example, 'The IIP Standard' or 'The Action Plan' or 'The Portfolio'. Smaller groups could report back to the whole group on their remit, *eg* appraisal system, or on their discussion, *eg* What do we need to know about assessment interviews? or on their practice session, *eg* How we managed to cope with the kinds of questions an assessor might ask us.

Other groups could operate as follows:

Formal remits – job descriptions, access to training documents of individuals

Discussion groups – when as a company do we think we would be ready for assessment?

Work groups – what types of training do we need to do our jobs effectively?

Managerial groups – how do we evaluate the effects of training on our production efforts towards achieving the business plan?

The main point is that every individual is really knowledgeable about Investors in People, especially as it applies to their job.

DEVELOPING POSITIVE ATTITUDES

Positive attitudes in a workforce are caused by job satisfaction, which in turn reflects good working conditions, the feelings of empowerment and responsibility, pride in one's organisation and the job one is doing, and recognition as an individual – all of which relate to being well trained in the job.

An organisation which achieves the Investors in People Standard will have employees with positive attitudes because they are seen as a vital ingredient in reaching shared business goals.

To underline the type of organisation which is most likely to be an Investor in People, consider the opposite, where the staff will have negative attitudes.

10 ways of not achieving Investors in People

1. No coherent business plan.
2. Lack of clear policy from the top.
3. Workforce unaware of anything except their own task.
4. Staff are expendable – plenty of people to replace them.
5. No interest in individuals or their abilities – just cogs in a wheel.
6. Training haphazard, misdirected and only as and when required.
7. Effects not evaluated.
8. No recruitment, selection or induction policy.
9. No training or development policy.
10. Staff work at jobs for which they are not trained.

Positive attitudes are also the result of **good leadership**. Just as commitment to Investors in People must come from the top so the qualities of good leadership can expedite and smooth the way to positive change.

Applying leadership

What do we know about leadership qualities and how can we apply such knowledge to an IIP programme? One individual who must have the qualities is the Investors in People organiser. And you must have **someone** doing this job. Someone has to plan and work towards the assessment procedure, no matter how much or little is required to reach it. He/she must of course have total support from the top. This also means time. If your organisation is not willing to invest in time and resources, it may well lack the enthusiasm which is required. The requirement for these need not be excessive but they must be sufficient to produce results.

Supposing your organisation has other quality programmes in mind or ongoing, *eg* ISO9000 or the Citizens Charter. You are asked to organise an IIP plan. You may ask yourself if there will be sufficient support to deal with these plans simultaneously. As you can imagine, it is the enthusiastic organisations which want to do everything. Should you proceed? It is really a matter of judgement. If it is thought that sufficient resources can be provided, then it may well be good policy to go ahead. Conversely, there can be confusions between different processes – although there are also overlaps which can be useful, *eg* the job descriptions required for ISO9000 are useful in deciding on induction programmes and in the appraisal of staff.

If your organisation has real leadership, it will be possible for it to over-achieve and to be, compared with the average, over-ambitious.

What is 'real' leadership?
Two kinds of leadership have been identified:

- The transactional
- The transformational.

The **transactional** leader is effective because he/she defines goals and tasks and rewards employees for their endeavours. Such a leader could be regarded as an able manager rather than a leader.

The **transformational** leader creates and communicates a vision of where the organisation is going and how it is going to succeed. He/she leads by example, showing the energy, drive and creativity expected of employees.

What type of person is the transformational leader?

Qualities	*How?*
Has charisma	By exemplifying vision
Shows individual consideration	By recognising people's strengths
Provides intellectual stimulation	By delegating challenging tasks

The transformational manager also:

- emphasises **goals** rather than method
- rewards **performance** and **effort**.

Although only a few people exhibit the almost indefinable quality of charisma, most of us can effectively bring about transformational change by:

- setting people clear objectives
- relating them to the leaders' vision of the future
- treating people as individuals
- recognising their needs to be responsible
- giving praise, recognition and tangible reward.

This is a real application of the much quoted views of McGregor and his X and Y theory of management. Undoubtedly his Y manager exhibits many of the necessary leadership qualities (transformations) which we have just described.

SUMMARY

- Communication – giving information to all employees is vital.
- Changes in culture, *eg* extending a training role to staff where training is not their main job.
- Action planning – must include specifics – who and when?
- The learning organisation – focusing on learning rather than instruction or training.
- Changes in role – is everyone pleased about this? Answering objections.
- Everyone must be included – individual training plans.
- Developing enthusiasm for Investors in People. Various ways of motivating people.

- Training and development as motivation.
- Leadership – transactional and transformational.

CASE STUDY

Ryan's big mistake

'So, Vernon', said Ryan, rather smugly, 'I think you'll have to agree I got on with the business at the speed of light.'

He had been describing the first meeting he had chaired of the Appraisal Working Group:

REMIT – 'To develop in detail, including organisation and documentation, a system for every employee to have an appraisal or development interview with his/her line manager.'

'We got through that agenda – and it's quite impressive, don't you think? – so quickly that they were out of the conference room in 30 minutes at most.'

He pushed the agenda over the desk to Vernon (who should have been sent a copy, for comment, in advance of the meeting). It read:

1. Remit of Working Group
2. Individual responsibilities for planning
   (a) setting out objectives of the appraisal system
   (b) appraisal interview forms
   (c) appraisal of managers (by staff) procedures
   (d) training of line managers to the appraisal
   (e) storage of appraisal information – confidentiality – access.
3. Pilot appraisals
   (a) target date
   (b) number involved.
4. Target dates for agenda items.

'Item 2(c) is a bit contentious, Ryan', declared Vernon. 'I really think that you should have asked me about it first – and this isn't the first time I've had to warn you about this. Even then I would have had to clear it with James Goodlad – it's risky.'

'Oh, rubbish,' shouted Ryan, 'nobody raised any objections at the meeting.' Weakly Vernon took the matter no further but decided that he would 'have a word' later. In the meantime, he agreed that the agenda contained many important ideas and things to do.

'And you had no problems in allocating these various tasks?'

'None at all.' (Although Vernon detected just a slight hint of doubt.)

'Oh, well, congratulations, looks as if you've done well.'

No sooner had Ryan departed than Vernon was aware of a tall figure standing hesitantly at his half-open door.

'Come in, please', he said, polite as ever.

In came Mike Smithers, a senior team leader and one of Ryan's Working Group.

'Sorry to trouble you, Vernon,' he muttered apologetically, 'but there is something I'd like to tell you about.'

As always, Vernon agreed to listen to Mike right away.

'Please sit down and go ahead', he said.

'Well it's about this appraisal working group.'

'Oh, yes.'

'Well, there are six of us, as you know, Ryan, Jim Hayes, the Operations Manager, Linda Cook of Marketing, Ron Swift, myself and Kimberley Todd representing the shop floor . . .. We were sure we would all have jobs to do – make a contribution to the Group's remit . . . enlist the help of our workmates.'

'Of course', agreed Vernon.

'Well, we didn't . . . Ryan says he will do draft documents on everything . . . and then we can comment on them – make some changes if we want. . . .'

As soon as Mike left, Vernon summoned Ryan. Of course Vernon had been against the IIP programme – it could take 18 months or two years . . . might stir things up a bit – so near to his own retirement. Here was just the kind of complication he had feared. He had given Ryan his head, however, and he appeared to have fallen at the first fence!

'Ryan,' he said, 'why on earth haven't you delegated some of these jobs on the Working Group's remit?'

'Oh, have they been complaining?'

'Not exactly, they just don't know why they're needed at all . . . feel that they've been dismissed as unimportant and incapable.'

'Oh, but they will be able to comment. Probably they're not up to all the ins and outs.'

'Nonsense,' snorted Vernon, 'the first law of personnel is to respect people – giving them a clear job to do and let them get on with it . . . Anyway, you can't possibly do the whole lot yourself effectively.'

'But, but,' stuttered Ryan, 'remember I said we wanted to keep it all in HRD.'

'You said so, but it's not on. If you really think that way, you're more stupid that I thought. Of course, we'll organise things, we'll chair meetings, if asked, keep the whole thing going along but we certainly won't run it all ourselves – a fatal error. Which reminds me, Clive Rawlinson, the consultant, will be here on Thursday. Take him round. Introduce him to everybody. Give him all the relevant company papers – the lot. Make sure he's really involved too. Then we'll discuss things with him. So go and reconvene that meeting. Tell them we've decided to delegate 100 per cent. I'm sure it will work out well. And, by the way, don't be ten minutes late the next time I send for you!'

Vernon began to warm to IIP.

Question

Do you agree that the 'professionals' must delegate jobs to different departments and employees at all levels in projects like Investors in People? Why in this instance? What benefit would accrue from delegation in addition to the feeling of 'involvement'?

DISCUSSION POINTS

1. Why do you think communication is so poor in so many organisations? Are some managers suspicious of too much open communication?

2. Is the idea of involving everybody unpopular with some management and staff? If so, why? Has it something to do with power?

3. Do motivation theories work in real life? Is it a purely cynical view that people are motivated only by fear, anxiety, money and ego?

4. Do you agree with the importance of leadership in bringing about change or in implementing any kind of strategic programme?

3
Writing the Action Plan

IDENTIFYING THE KEY TASKS

Diagnostic assessments

You have already been able to find out from the Short Questionnaire, Assessing Your Own Attitudes, in Chapter 1, whether you should proceed to IIP, whether your business strategy fits with the requirements of the Standard.

You have also, as a result of using diagnostic assessment with a few key managers, completed an audit of where your organisation is at present placed on its journey towards recognition.

In this chapter we will combine:

- details of where you are on all the Indicators
- how you score overall on the Indicators
- awareness of how management's views on these are similar to or different from those of the workforce

and use all this information in the construction of an Investors in People Action Plan.

Diagnostic questionnaires

The Investors in People Standard, Section 6, Evidence Guide, quotes the Principles and Indicators, and for each of the latter provides useful information under three headings, Guidance, Key Questions and Evidence, *eg*:

Indicator 3.3. All employees are made aware of the development opportunities open to them.

Guidance
eg This indicators puts the onus on the employer to communicate development opportunities open to them.

Key questions
What information and advice on training, development and job opportunities are available to employees?

Typical evidence
eg Results of employee survey.

The **Diagnostic Pack (Scotland)** consists, as we have seen, of 81 questions, each of which can be answered Yes (10 points); Partly true (5 points) and No (0 points).

It is very useful in identifying specific indicators which still have to be covered adequately, and, of course, any of the four main principles which still require a good deal of detailed consideration.

The **Development Workbook (Scotland)** is doubly useful because it acts both as an explanatory document of what is meant by an assessment indicator and also asks questions regarding what your organisation does now in relation to each of them:

- What happens in this organisation?
- How do you know that this happens effectively?
- Does documentation exist to demonstrate this? If, so, what?

Very usefully, for your action plan, you can use the information you have obtained to complete the first column (see page 47).

None of these questionnaires/guides should be thought of as in any way mysterious. One very quick and insightful way of taking a quick audit of your organisation's present position in relation to the IIP assessment indicators is simply to turn each statement into a question, *eg*:

Indicator 4.3. The outcome of training and development are evaluated at individual, team and organisational level.

becomes

Do we evaluate the outcome of training at

- *individual*
- *team*
- *organisational levels?*

Subsidiary questions on how and by whom can wait until your small management groups agree on Yes, No or Partly true. Whatever your result, it is likely you **will** agree you **should** be able to say they **are** done.

SURVEYING TRAINING NEEDS

If you work for a larger organisation of around 200 employees (or fewer if you really want a wide, overall viewpoint) it will be an advantage to carry out a staff survey to ensure you know the views of virtually everyone in the business – how they think your organisation stands in terms of the IIP indicators. If the whole staff is too large a number to cope with, distribute survey questionnaires to a sample, *eg* 25 per cent of the whole group, with sub-groups represented proportionately.

Excellent questionnaires to use for this purpose when working with a TEC would be the Review Tools provided in *How to Become an Investor in People* (see Further Reading). Separate forms are provided for Top Management and All Employees (General).

Each question is matched to a particular indicator or indicators. If you believe you are weaker in one of the principles than others, you could compose supplementary questions of your own to cover the relevant indicators more completely. To take one example:

COMMITMENT
Circle the letter which corresponds to your opinion of what happens in your organisation.

Indicator 1.5 is covered (for Management) by –

Statement 8: We have communicated to our employees what they need to do to help the organisation succeed. A B C D *

and (for General – all staff) –

Statement 4: I understand what I need to do to help the organisation succeed. A B C D *

A Always applies/happens/we have done this
B Quite often applies/happens
C Rarely applies/happens
D Never applies (or we have not done this)

* *Note*: If you have detailed information from now obsolete 'Toolboxes' it should still be very useful in developing an action plan.

Results

With both survey questionnaires, calculating the percentage of ABCD responses can provide you with:

- An estimate of the relevant strengths of your organisation on the four principles.
- A comparison of the views of management with those of other staff on the amount of progress already made or still to be made on specific process (often Management responses are more optimistic).

If you are working with a LEC in Scotland, you could use the survey questionnaire contained in the Development Workbook (Scotland). This is also an excellent device for obtaining the views of a whole staff or a representative sample. Some questions are specifically for different groups of staff, including those with different types of job or lengths of employment within the organisation. Again, the amount of agreement/disagreement between the responses of different groups can help identify any serious gaps in meeting the criteria of the indicators.

Extra information

When issuing questionnaires to staff it can be a good opportunity to ask some questions of your own, *eg*:

1. What specific training have you yourself had in the last six months? (A way of checking official records.)
2. What type of course (including VQ qualifications) would you like in the next six months?
3. Why do you regard training as important to you? Tick one box.
   Improving job performance ❐
   Coping with new processes ❐
   Gaining promotion ❐
   Boosting self-confidence ❐

Communication

Before issuing questionnaire-type forms to employees/managers, you should act on the following points:

- Explain why you are issuing the questionnaire.

- Assure staff that responses will be anonymous.
- Promise that information on results will be issued to all participants.
- Guarantee that action will be taken on the results.
- Begin to consider the need for portfolio evidence of systems being in place. If questionnaire results have been reassuring on, for example, induction processes, indicate that documents are available on a Matrix set out in similar format to that on page 114. This will enable you to make a really effective start on a process which can continue through the Assessment Process to Reassessment and Re-recognition.

SETTING OBJECTIVES

Just as setting objectives is important for your business in general so also is it a vital process of your IIP strategy. As already noted, some TECs and LECs either advise or insist that you have an action plan in place before you embark on a programme. This is really common sense since we are considering a timescale which could last anywhere between six months and two years or more, depending on your starting point and the resources available. If you have disagreements at the beginning on whether certain criteria have been achieved or not, do more work on them until there is general positive agreement amongst your working group.

Assume that you have ascertained from the diagnostic assessments and/or from a survey those processes and systems which are in place, those which exist in part, and those which have still to be developed. Assume also that you do not have a process for identifying individual training needs such as an appraisal system. Then you should make immediate and strenuous efforts to start such a process so as to have it embedded within your organisation before the IIP assessment. From the start also, arrange for such a system to contain an evaluation device, *eg* a questionnaire for employees and managers/team leaders on its effectiveness.

Just having the mechanics of appraisal is not enough. It must be seen by both top management and employees as being well established and helpful as well as practical and realistic. Indeed this should be true of your whole Investors System.

Objectives, therefore, are identified by studying the difference between the present situation and the achievement of the processes required to bridge the gap. 'Action required' is your way of reaching these objectives.

DELEGATING RESPONSIBILITY

As to the action plan itself, it is essentially a series of systematic objectives defined by 'Action required' – a plan of campaign towards achieving the Standard. There will be a permanent IIP Working Group, planning for both Assessment/Recognition and later Re-assessment/Re-recognition. It will certainly not be the responsibility of HRD/Personnel staff alone. The group will delegate individuals or sub-groups to push ahead with the practical organisation; for example, induction processes, publicising training opportunities, evaluating training and developing, or devising a staff selection system. An individual or a group could be responsible for the collection and collation of documentary or other evidence for the Portfolio. The whole Working Group must also have a senior manager as the overall co-ordinator of the system. He/she could be the head of HRD or a senior manager, especially in smaller organisation, and certainly with a very good picture of the whole organisation.

PLANNING SYSTEMATICALLY

The best way to start planning is for each member of your IIP Working Group to have a drafting paper with headings for each of five columns.

As an example, how would you start planning for assessment indicator 1.5?

> *The employer has considered what employees at all levels will contribute to the organisation and has communicated this effectively to them.*

Assume that you already have a clear mission statement which summarises for employees and customers what your organisation aims to achieve, for example:

> 'Through effective leadership and management to inspire every member of staff to supply the customer with quality products at the most competitive prices.'

Now there is a need for more precise detail. Remember when writing the Action Plan to make your intentions as clear as possible. Use precise verbs and set meaningful, realistic targets. Ensure that specific people are nominated to carry out the tasks. Give them adequate time, remembering that many people are over-optimistic at first about time required. On the other hand, too long a target completion period can lead to tasks being put off for too long.

Discussion amongst the Working Group leads to this plan.

Indicator 1.5

Present situation	**Action required**	**Persons responsible**	**Target completion time**
Employees are all aware of the mission statement. Senior management have drawn up a business plan and identified training needs departmentally.	All staff to be issued with the mission statement and business plan (or short version). Top management to give presentations to all staff on essentials of the business plan as stemming out from the mission statement. Specific departmental contributions are highlighted. Line managers to discuss with teams at appraisals and group meetings (minutes to be circulated). HRD to organise short course for line managers on discussing the plan at appraisals and team meetings.	Induction working group. HRD to liaise with top management and line managers. HRD to organise short course for line managers on how to communicate their department's/team's objectives to new staff. The relevant VQs will also be discussed.	10.02.9X

As another example, take indicator 3.1:

> *All new employees are introduced effectively to the organisation and are given the training and development they need to do the job.*

Assume that you have an elementary but not very systematic induction procedure. Further discussion produces a decision for a member of the Working Group to form an induction sub group which will carry out the following remit in detail:

Indicator 3.1

Present situation	Action required	Persons responsible	Target completion time
New employees are introduced to their line manager and other staff in the same department/area. Line manager ascertains training needs. No induction to business as a whole.	Expand induction, *eg* presentations on aims of whole business. Arrange a sequential programme with objectives relating to business as a whole, department and teams. Ask existing employees about improvements which could be made. Revise personal development forms and formulate questionnaire for evaluating inductions.	Induction Working Group.	02.04.9X

Covering indicators thoroughly

Fourteen assessment indicators (1.5, 2.2, 2.3, 2.4, 2.5, 2.6, 3.2, 3.3, 3.4, 3.5, 3.6, 4.1, 4.2, 4.3) could all relate to an appraisal process but the latter is not the *only* basis for ensuring a complete coverage of them all. It is probably wise to have three pieces of evidence for each indicator. What types of evidence may be useful and which could be included in your action plan?

We shall take one example from each principle (except 1.5, covered previously).

> *2.2 Training and development needs are regularly reviewed against business objectives.*

Present situation	Action required	Persons responsible	Target completion time
Basic appraisal system in place.	Develop survey forms on training needs for various groups. Methodology for	'x' to co-ordinate sub group on survey and training	09.04.9X

	analysis of results to be devised.	needs analysis.	

3.3 All employees are made aware of development opportunities open to them.

Present situation	Action required	Persons responsible	Target completion time
Basic appraisal system in place.	Noticeboards or monitors to be increased to ensure *all* employees can see them.	'z' to investigate and report back costs.	05.06.9X
	Group to be set up to develop newsletter mainly about training opportunities and staff success.	Sub group co-ordinated by 'y'.	10.05.9X
	Managers to be instructed to include training and development needs and opportunities to be permanent items on team meeting agendas.	Managers/team leaders	

4.3 The outcomes of training and development are evaluated at individual, team and organisational level.

Present situation	Action required	Persons responsible	Target completion time
Basic appraisal system in place.	All staff to complete questionnaire feedback forms after all courses.	'x' to construct feedback questionnaire.	01.07.9X
	Staff to discuss courses with their line managers before and after – objectives – were they achieved? Managers to collate these reports. Central co-ordinator to collate all objectives	'y' to collect all line managers' reports and summarise for senior management annually.	01.07.9X

and evaluation forms
and report to directors/
senior management.
Teams to discuss
group learning
processes and evaluation
discussions to be
summarised and
sent to co-ordinator.
Forms to be devised.
Check on whether
individual objectives
set at appraisal have
been achieved.

SETTING PRIORITIES

Some of the processes which are really important and worthwhile within the IIP process, such as **induction, appraisal** and **evaluation**, would have to be given priority status in your action planning, especially if a great deal needed to be done. The scheduling of the action plan's details depends on the level of development of these processes and their relative urgency.

On the other hand, it is very useful to think of the Investors process as an ever-evolving one rather than the setting-up of an immediate, short-term 'experiment' to cover IIP requirements.

Remember, all the procedures are good for your organisation's needs on a permanent basis.

PLANNING FLEXIBLY

You should also regard the action plan as a flexible process. Necessary 'actions' can change or vary according to the developmental stage reached for each of the criteria. So also can time limits. Some will turn out to be either too optimistic or pessimistic. Some processes will be seen in a different light – as easier or more difficult than expected – or as requiring more work in relation to other processes, as one influences the other. Priorities will also depend on the availability of staff and/or the consultant to provide inputs into new processes. Try to involve as many staff as possible at all levels of your business.

Remember, the whole process requires tenacity to keep going along with other necessary jobs connected with your work.

INVESTING IN PEOPLE AS A PROCESS

Most diagrams show IIP as a one-way step-by-step process from commitment to evaluation. Before committing, an organisation should construct an action plan to check feasibility and what will have to be done. If groups or individuals are then asked to plan and implement each of the processes (or stages), they must constantly interact, *eg.* the planned objectives of the processes of induction and appraisal can be applied to evaluate their effectiveness. On this basis, Evaluation can be planned at the same time as the other processes. The whole evaluation process can then point to changes which can be made, *eg* directed back to Review, and if evaluation is really negative, to Commitment.

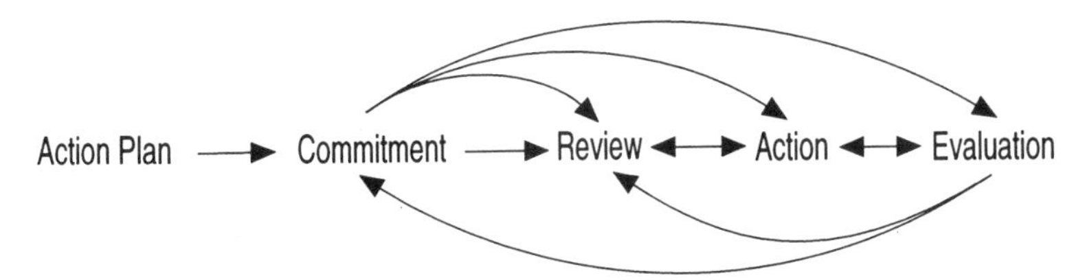

Fig. 2. Investing in people as a process.

SUMMARY

- Assessments which indicate your organisation's readiness for Investors in People are listed.
- Surveys of training needs which are completed by employees also help to pinpoint training and development needs from the employees' point of view.
- How to set IIP objectives, including who and when, is covered.
- Examples of action planning are provided.
- Changes in action plans, according to progress, can be made.

CASE STUDY

Alex lays down the law

'We really must make up our minds in our priorities in the action plan', observed Alex Thomson-Bell.

In the two weeks since she had decided to proceed with an Investors Programme she had quickly contacted her local TEC, read her way through the Standard, completed the 33 item questionnaire for Management, and had asked two of her senior colleagues to do the same.

Alex had answered the 25 questions on her own and had arrived at a very optimistic score. Her PA, Ruth Trotter, had also made, by sheer chance of course, an identical score. The two senior staff, Mary Hughes and Phillip Rawlinson, agreed on a more cautious estimate and the other staff members had mulled over the 17 questions (general) and had, anonymously, returned results which were even more cautious than Mary and Phillip's.

Everyone, even Alex, agreed that the two most urgent areas were on discussions about training needs and evaluation. It was doubtful, to say the least, whether everyone really did have regular discussions with their manager, either Mary or Phillip, or the latter two with Alex.

Only Alex thought that after training had been completed that *she* reviewed the benefits to the business and the individual.

'Of course I know what's happening all the time', she pronounced. Ruth agreed eagerly with this.

'I think', said Phillip, 'we need to put a lot of thought into this tricky business of evaluating the training we do.'

'Nonsense', snorted Alex, 'all we need is a really tough appraisal system where we can check on training needed and the effects of previous training. If there's been no effect we tell them off for it.'

(No one agreed with Alex that 'appraisals' in the IIP sense were disciplining devices.)

'Well', said Ruth timidly, 'why don't we concentrate on appraisals *and* evaluation?'

'OK', snapped Alex, 'you, Ruth, will work with Will Brown [an unpromoted employee] on appraisals while Phillip and Mary will do evaluation. I'll try to join you on evaluation as often as possible. We must finish both of these in a fortnight. It won't be too difficult because we really do it all already. Oh, and I've changed my mind about MBAs. I'm going to make up a learning programme for myself based on short courses and conferences for myself. Ruth will do a PA course at the FE college and everyone else will do either the part-time course on Advanced Design at the university or the level 2 VQ on Interior Design.'

'This doesn't leave us very much to decide for ourselves', whispered Phillip to Mary.

'I agree, but wait till the appraisals start – we'll at least be able to suggest and write down other possible courses which would be more relevant', replied Mary, '*and* it may be difficult for Alex to contradict them if we make a really good case that they're best for the business.'

Question

List all the mistakes made by Alex Thomson-Bell during the staff meeting and any plus points.

What improvements could be made in the way the meeting was handled and on the decisions made? Compare your observations with those put forward in the Case Study and Discussion section.

DISCUSSION POINTS

1. Is an action plan particularly necessary in view of all the changes you may have to make in scheduling because of other demands on you and your IIP Working Group? Wouldn't it be equally effective to work on the main requirements for your organisation and pick up the other planning details later?

2. Should the action plan cover every one of the indicators or only those which you definitely think require to be covered because they do not have processes or evidence in place already?

3. Should individuals or groups scheduled to work on specific processes make sure that they will have materials available for the portfolio (*eg* forms relating to inductions or appraisals)? Or should this be another person's or group's responsibility?

4. If you found that a few individuals or groups were not completing their action plan tasks on time, how best should you deal with this problem?

5. Should all employees be given a copy of the action plan so that they know exactly who is doing what?

4
Achieving Investors in People: Committing

We start by quoting the first of the four principles of IIP and the two statements stemming from it.

> *An Investor in People makes a public commitment from the top to develop all employees to achieve its business objectives.*
>
> Every employer should have a written but flexible plan which sets out business goals and targets, considers how employees will contribute to achieving the plan and specifies how development needs in particular will be assessed and met.
>
> Management should develop and communicate to all employees a vision of where the organisation is going and the contribution employees will make to its success, including employee representatives as appropriate.

The **method** we shall use in considering the practical aspects of IIP is to:

- quote each indicator
- make general points about how you should set about meeting it
- detail specific steps.

GETTING COMMITMENT AT SENIOR LEVEL

> **1.1 There is a public commitment from the most senior level within the organisation to develop people.**

Unless your organisation is quite small and decisions are made quickly because few people are involved, you will have to obtain support for an Investors programme from the people at the top – the board, chief executive or managing director plus other senior managers. You may be able to obtain such support quite easily. On the other hand you may have to persuade decision-makers that IIP is a highly positive long-term strategy.

How can you persuade them to give you the go-ahead?

- Be enthusiastic.
- Explain the basic aims and principles.
- List the solid benefits.
- Benchmark the achievements of other organisations with IIP in the same sector.
- Express your personal views that the benefits far outweigh costs.
- List your estimated costs, including assessment fees.
- Answer critical questions factually and pleasantly.

First practical steps

Assume that you have obtained the positive endorsement of top management and the board and you can now proceed. You are committed. What next?

After consulting with top management and a range of staff, you should establish an Investors in People working group – up to ten people, at various levels, representing most divisions and departments. The remit is to organise a programme which will enable the organisation to reach the IIP standard within a flexible time limit, minimum six months, maximum 24 months.

The group will have the ability to meet quite frequently. Its initial spadework is to:

- **read** the principles and indicators carefully
- **diagnose** your current situation in relation to IIP
- **construct** an action plan
- **plan** the delegation of various tasks to members of the working group and to line managers.

Announcing the plan
In the meantime you have discussed with the senior management how to inform all employees of IIP and of the programme to be followed in general. This can be done by arranging meetings, some large, some of small groups. Talks on which senior management are involved can be given on the IIP Standard and what is involved in reaching it. Sub groups within the larger meetings can then discuss the various aspects such as the four principles, appraisals and induction, the action plan, evaluation, the portfolio, and how IIP is assessed.

Issuing papers
At the same meetings, the mission statement of the organisation and the business plan, or extracts from it, and details of the IIP Standard should be issued to all staff. These should also be covered by explanatory talks. Senior management will know that a **business plan** is the only **compulsory** document which has to be provided during the assessment process. They will also be aware that for a company to rely only upon such a small amount of written evidence would be a mistake. Other supporting documents will help to provide evidence that your organisation meets all the assessment indicators for Investors in People recognition.

COMMITMENT: MEANING AND DETAILS

We shall now look at each of the **commitment indicators** in turn so that you know exactly what they are about and what you need to know and do.

Recall that indicator 1.1 stated that **There is a public commitment from the most senior level within the organisation to develop people.**

A public commitment means that now that you have successfully persuaded the board and directors that they should endorse Investors in People enthusiastically, the next important issue is that all employees must know about the commitment, what it is all about and what action will be taken.

Staff must feel confident that the organisation is committed to people development and that there will be equal opportunities within the procedures.

The organisation's commitment must be set down in writing, including a letter of commitment to the chief executive of the Training and Enterprise/Local Enterprise Company.

In it you should state your beliefs in the importance of the four principles and in the training and development of people. You regard this development as an investment in your employees, the most important of all your resources.

The TEC/LEC's chief executive will acknowledge your letter. The two letters should be included within your company's **portfolio of evidence**, which is part of your assessment process. It is a good habit to learn to keep a copy of every document which may be of relevance, *eg* internal memos and course evaluation.

You may also be able to display a 'Statement of Commitment' within your premises.

It should be emphasised to employees — and note that 'employee' means everyone, including part-time staff – that they do not need to memorise documents such as the IIP Standard but they should be generally aware of them.

In future they will be made aware of progress towards the Standard and about training needs and courses which have been organised to achieve the company's vision, aims and objectives.

Awareness should also include the specific objectives to be reached, the profitability of the organisation and improvements in performance which are due to the Investors in People programme.

Public communication of this kind – and its importance cannot be emphasised enough – is like an extra fifth principle of Investors in People.

It can be helped through devices such as:

- newsletters
- noticeboards
- staff announcement systems
- team, departmental and larger meetings.

Keeping records

A record of discussion or minute of meetings should be kept, especially of those dealing with training and development needs.

All staff should be aware of how their team or they, as individuals, are contributing towards reaching business goals:

- in production generally
- in specific project work
- in profitability.

ACHIEVING A COMMON VISION

1.2 Employees at all levels are aware of the broad aims or vision of the organisation.

Before you start your IIP programme it is important that employees know the main purposes of your organisation. This is the best way to focus the efforts of all staff and to develop a sense of pride throughout the workforce. A mission statement is an excellent way of expressing the philosophy of your business. How would you write one for your organisation?

You could well start with the needs of your customers, *eg*:

- supplying quality goods
- providing excellent service
- meeting the customers' requirements
- delivering on time or well within time
- value for money.

Along with these, you should also have aims for internal company development, *eg*:

- motivating people through good pay levels and intrinsic satisfaction with the job
- emphasising the training and development of employees
- evaluating investment in training and development
- setting targets for continuous improvement
- communicating business goals and progress towards them.

These are examples only. Of course, you should write down exactly what your organisation tries to do.

The next step is to **summarise** all your aims into a short statement. It could be one or several sentences (see Figure 3). The main requirement is for the workforce to remember it and use it as encapsulating the vision of the organisation. Each vital activity, therefore, should be part of the mission statement.

The message, to make an impact, must be:

- brief
- clear
- memorable.

So, knowledge of the **mission statement** will help towards motivation and IIP awareness but something more is needed.

Vision also represents the leadership qualities of the management team as a whole. How far have they conveyed a clear idea of the positive future of the organisation? Translating this into reality means:

- giving staff a clear, straightforward version of the business plan and mission statement
- discussing details of the plan in relation to the team at its regular meetings
- explaining to each employee his/her role in meeting the aims of the business plan
- giving every staff member, full or part-time, a copy of their job description and going through it with them in detail. This applies at management as well as other levels of staff.

Our mission is to:
Meet our customers' needs through providing excellent goods and services at value for money prices and on time.

We will ensure these high standards through:

motivating our staff by rewarding them well through first class working conditions and pay, supported by a well organised training and development programme, clear individual and team goals and enlightened, efficient leadership motivated towards continuing improvement.

Fig. 3. Example of a mission statement.

DRAWING UP A BUSINESS PLAN

> **1.3 There is a written but flexible plan which sets out business goals and targets.**

The **business plan** itself should cover a period varying from three to five years. The longer the time, the more general the targets will be.

Who writes the plan?

As suggested in this book, the senior management team can deal with the plan's general business aims and strategies and each head of division/department will set down his/her group's objectives relative to the overall plan. This would include the human resources senior manager, who will specify in some detail how training and development needs may be established through:

- a survey of employees
- a training needs analysis.

As part of the plan, the HRD manager, or equivalent in the smaller organisation, will be able, through a written policy statement, to provide managers with guidance on procedures for arranging training, including access to the training budget. Even details like the completion of forms, *eg* to apply for training, to evaluate courses, to be a record of individual group and/or team training, will be well worthwhile.

What to say in your business plan

The business plan, as it appears in your portfolio, does not need to be a very long document. If the full version is both detailed and lengthy, what you put in the portfolio would be ideally an **accurate summary** from which the assessor can identify the essential message in quite a short time.

Even the name 'business plan' should not deter you. Many organisations have a document which sets out what they hope to do in future, even if it is only a projection in an annual report. In cases like this, if you have the main objectives listed, it would be desirable to expand it into more detail, including training required.

What you need to do essentially is to say what your business objectives are, how you are going to achieve them (especially through training and development), and how you will evaluate progress.

You can include financial or production data but remember that the main reasons for it are practical ones and that such data should be the bases for future targets. You should compose the plan with these and your mission statement in mind.

How should you set about writing the plan? First, set down your main headings:

- quote the mission statement
- set down the main objectives (five to ten) deriving from the statement, *eg:*

  (1) to increase production of . . . by . . .% within . . . months/years

  (2) to increase profits to £ . . . by . . . years

  (3) to increase the business through the development of new
    (a) products
    (b) services

  (4) to provide training courses for staff in line with the Mission Statement and the objectives for 199X, linked to National/Scottish Vocational Qualifications.

The details of the plan can be provided by each director and senior manager writing down the specifics for his/her division. For details of all the VQs available look at:

- The NVQ Monitor (NCVQ, see Useful Addresses)
- SVQ Update (SCOTVEC), see Useful Addresses).

In addition to the targets/objectives, they will also set down the training and development processes required by themselves, managers, supervisors and all staff.

In addition to training required for the **technicalities** of each job, some employees will need more general training, *eg* management staff will need courses on:

- appraising staff
- identifying training needs
- monitoring and evaluating progress

- interviewing
- carrying out surveys
- awareness of NVQs/SVQs and other relevant qualifications
- team leadership
- staff recruitment, selection and induction.

VQ qualifications in Management (Management Charter Initiative) and in Training, Assessment and Verification could all be of interest to you as your own staff could become qualified and be involved in internal training and assessment. TECs and LECs as well as the Institute of Personnel and Development, City and Guilds, SCOTVEC, The Open College, RSA, local colleges and training organisations could advise you on these awards.

Once each manager of each department has contributed to the plan, the whole document should be brought together and edited.

All line managers would then identify who on their staff needed what type of training. Individual or team courses, qualifying or otherwise, could be arranged internally or externally. The aims, objectives and contents of these courses/training exercises could be discussed during departmental and team meetings at individual training meetings and during the more formal appraisal interviews.

IDENTIFYING DEVELOPMENT NEEDS

1.4 The plan identifies broad development needs and specifies how they will be assessed and met.

This criterion is covered by the section in the business plan dealing with overall **training needs**. The plan should specify the types of training required for each group, division or team and the qualifications – ranging from MBAs to VQs. It may be possible for line managers or other staff to carry out the training themselves and they themselves may be involved in taking VQs or other qualifications in mentoring, training, development and assessment.

It may be difficult to anticipate every training need but reasonable guesses can be made including cost of training. 'Costs' here may also represent time used by existing employees on training or coaching other members of the workforce. Again, note that courses can range from the formal/external type to informal coaching or mentoring by other employees, not necessarily training experts – more likely line managers.

IDENTIFYING THE ROLE OF INDIVIDUALS

> **1.5 The employer has considered what employees, at all levels, will contribute to the success of the organisation, and has communicated this effectively to them.**

Even if staff are really aware of the mission statement and business plan, more detail is needed to cover this assessment indicator. Individually, staff can have job descriptions and their own training plan and records. This lets them see how their role fits into the plan. Teams, through meetings and briefings, will know what they are expected to do. Through staff suggestion schemes for improvement and meetings based on an empowerment approach, they can put forward their ideas on how to promote quality and achieve the aims of the business plan.

Measuring employee success

Although employees can be aware of the general objectives of the business, one of the big problems for larger organisations, especially if involved in manufacturing, is how to let each individual see how they are contributing. If a departmental target for production has been set, then this can be quantified in terms of individual objectives, *eg* producing (x) widgets per shift, with a reject rate calculated in terms of the group's quality objectives.

Attendance/absentee rates can also be set for a specific group of employees.

Yet another individual or group target would be in terms of saving through increased quality or through expenditure savings or savings in production time suggested by empowered groups who can see such possibilities much better than managers. Groups can later see if these targets have been met. Being able to relate such successes to new processes will be particularly effective in achieving IIP.

Yet another way of establishing and communicating training needs as seen by the workforce is the organisational survey. If it provides information on the views of all staff, it can be compared with the equivalent judgements of management. Normally there is a close correspondence between the two but quite often there can also be a significant disparity. Part of your IIP strategy can be the aim of bringing these two sets of views into alignment.

COMMUNICATING WITH EMPLOYEES

> **1.6 Where representative structures exist, management communicates with employee representatives a vision of where the organisation is going and the contribution employees (and their representatives) will make to its success.**

Unions will also be officially informed of the business plan and its associated training programme by management. Management can seek advice from the unions on such development programmes. The contribution union officials can make to the success of the IIP strategy should also be discussed. Regular meetings should include the Investors in People programme on the agenda and, again, records of consideration of Investors in People would be a helpful addition to the portfolio.

SUMMARY

In this chapter we have surveyed the principle of commitment and the assessment indicators dealing with:

- commitment at senior level
- achieving a common vision for the organisation
- drawing up a written but flexible business plan
- identifying broad development needs and meeting them
- communicating to employees their contributions to the business
- communicating with employee representatives.

CASE STUDY

Ken's persuasion wins

'As you were the only group of colleagues not to vote for IIP,' observed

Ken Hill, 'I just wanted to check again to see if you had changed your minds.

'Phil has written out an action plan, as you know – in fact you'll have been all given a copy – and it's been approved by everyone else, so now I would like to send in our letter of commitment. Have you by any chance just forgotten to let me know – because you have been very busy with the BFR (Business for Regeneration) documentation?'

'Oh no, we haven't been held up on that because we are too busy', replied Nora Thomson. 'We're not really convinced that you are committed to the idea of the training and development of staff.'

'How on earth not?', protested Ken. 'No one has ever been refused an application to go on a course, especially if it has been mulled over and discussed at our weekly group meeting.'

'Oh no, it's not that', spoke up Jaquie Gibson, 'we appreciate your support in the past. Now we believe that there's a subversive element.'

'But that is not being rational', protested Ken. 'You've had internal training for VQs, external training in assertiveness and two constructive appraisals already. What more can we do – where did we go wrong?'

'Well, it isn't really you', said the other staff member, Janet Scott, 'it's the wording of IIP.'

'Oh, in what way?'

'Well', continued Janet, 'it keeps saying that training and development should always be directed towards the aims set down in the business plan.'

'And so?' added Ken.

'Well, we think there's a possibility that there may be an ulterior motive – that it's not for our benefit but only in the interests of the business.'

Ken was quite shocked.

'Not at all,' he argued, 'quite often a course which was essentially about your personal development could be regarded as relating to our aims as a business – you wouldn't turn that idea down just because it wasn't 100 per cent employee and 0 per cent business.

'And you know about the views of some of the business gurus that companies should support training for very practical reasons, that is, it will help employees if by unfortunate circumstances they're made redundant at a later date. And, looking at it from the other side, training in relevant skills could lead to a business losing the very staff it had supported for training.'

'Well', said Nora, 'I can see that there *are* two sides to it.'

'I assure you – there are no snags attaching to IIP', said Ken reassuringly. 'Let's say that it's for the all round benefit of everyone.

'Can I take it that you are agreeable now to that letter of commitment being sent off today?'

There were nods all round. Ken felt a great sense of relief and some pride in his diplomacy.

Question

If you were confronted with this particular type of doubt, would you deal with it in the same way? What alternative approaches would you take? Are there other relevant points for IIP to put forward?

DISCUSSION POINTS

1. Why is it important that an organisation makes a formal commitment to the principles of IIP to the TEC/LECs?

2. Why should a business plan be the only totally compulsory document for an organisation aiming for IIP?

3. Do you think that it is really possible for an organisation to enable every employee to know how he/she contributes to the aims of the business plan? Are job descriptions enough in themselves?

4. Why is the wording of a mission statement regarded by successful companies as a vital part of business planning?

5
Achieving Investors in People: Planning/Reviewing

This chapter starts with direct quotations from the Standard – the second principle and two statements stemming out from it. The important process of appraising employees' training needs will be covered during the consideration of the indicators.

> *An Investor in People regularly reviews the needs and plans the training and development of all employees.*
>
> The resources for training and developing employees should be clearly identified in the business plan.
>
> Managers should be responsible for regularly agreeing training and development needs with each employee in the context of business objectives, setting targets and standards linked, where appropriate, to the achievement of National Vocational Qualifications (or relevant units), and in Scotland, Scottish Vocational Qualifications.

RESOURCING THE PLAN

> **2.1 The written plan identifies the resources that will be used to meet training and development needs.**

The main resources required for IIP are:

- money (training budgets)
- time (for training)
- employees (trainers)
- facilities.

Costing Investors in People

One of the most usually asked questions by organisations which are thinking about working towards Investors in People is 'How much is it going to cost?'

The answer depends very much on the views of the management involved. To some, the cost is only the fee charged for assessment, £550.00 per day of the assessor's time. To others it is the cost of the employees' training and the time required. The first of these two groups may already have an extensive training programme and the second very little at all. A change of strategy will therefore cost the second one more, but the positive effects will be all the greater.

Note that indicator 2.1 states that the business plan is **written**. It is also partly covered by the 1.1 to 1.4 indicators in the Commitment section.

Budgeting for training

For Investors in People the provision of an adequate training budget is very positive evidence. If an organisation **does not** have such a budget, it has to prove that it **does** fund essential group and individual training. In fact, details of the budget and proposed allocation arrangements should be included in the business plan. If there is no budget, a statement regarding availability of funding should be made in the plan.

Providing time

Time is another vital resource. If an employee attends a weekly one day release course, the wage he/she is paid for that day is, along with the fees, a resource. Additionally, the employer has to do without that employee's contribution to the business for one fifth or 20 per cent of the time during the period of the course involved.

Surveying employee skills

Then there are **employee resources**. What are the strengths of your workforce as a whole? How can they contribute to an IIP programme?

- Do they have experience as trainers, instructors or mentors?

- Do they have qualifications you don't know about?

It is quite possible to find well qualified people working at jobs which are well below the level of their qualifications. Surveys of your staff can include details of the additional skills of employees not previously known to the employer. This is an important point to check.

Identifying VQs

What types of training will be required – now and in the future? Managers will have to familiarise themselves with qualifications such as **Vocational Qualifications**, now being devised at rapid speed by representatives of all the different industries and occupations. Specific VQs are under development as well as other which are cross-job, multi-skill qualifications.

In the training and development section of an organisation's business plan, senior managers should be able to identify not just precise training needs but also the qualifications, at the appropriate levels which match the jobs.

Similarly, sub-managers and supervisors should be able to identify qualifications for their staff. Specific industries such as the chemical industry, through their lead bodies, will have relevant VQs, whilst trainers and line managers can work towards achieving training and development qualifications.

Counselling for careers

Yet another role which may be identified in your existing staff is the **career counsellor**. Employees at all levels may not see the way forward within a particular organisation. If they leave, this means potential talent is lost. A career counsellor can listen to their aspirations. He/she can discuss with them whether these hopes are realistic or not, assess any obstacles in the way and help them plan how to achieve qualifications that will enable them to move up or transfer to another role within the organisation. Such talent identification can lead to effective succession planning.

Using training facilities

Although emphasis is now placed on training, coaching and assessment taking place on the shop floor, **facilities** are still a valuable asset for larger organisations. Training rooms, videos and computer facilities can be supported by the traditional methods of instruction, such as books and other publications, distance learning material in the form of borrowable library facilities, etc. The availability of these within a resource centre will also help in the Investors in People programme.

MATCHING NEEDS TO OBJECTIVES

> **2.2 Training and development needs are regularly reviewed against business objectives.**

Matching training to business needs

One of the simplest but most effective of the IIP strategies is to relate training and development to the objectives of the organisation and its business plan. The idea seems childishly obvious but until the recent past many saw training as being a good thing in itself. Whoever actually went through a training process may well have been someone who was able to do it or could be spared. No attempt was made to see that the line manager and employee agreed on the need for the training or that the employee should know exactly why he/she needed it. Consequently the process of evaluation – finding out whether the training had been worth while – could not be carried out because no objectives had been set.

Training needs should be reviewed regularly at senior management, team and individual levels. Training and development should be a permanent item on the agenda at senior staff meetings and conclusions minuted (again useful for your portfolio).

Developing senior staff

Directors and senior managers should consider **their** development needs as well as the rest of the staff. They should at least have a **personal development plan**, involving, for example, strategic planning, personal effectiveness, chairing meetings, developing first rate leadership skills, awareness of the potential of new technology, listening skills and self-presentation.

Should directors or senior managers be appraised? If they do decide to go ahead with such a process, it would help to allay suspicions and anxieties from the workforce that such approaches must contain some kind of negative, hidden agenda if they are not also applied to senior members of staff.

Team discussions

Managers, either meeting together or with their own staff, should also discuss training needs in relation to the business plan or for new requirements arising from recent amendments to the plan. Perhaps the most urgent of such changes are those which derive from

- customer suggestions
- new opportunities to increase competitiveness.

REVIEWING TRAINING NEEDS

2.3 A process exists for regularly reviewing the training and development needs of all employees.

In looking at this assessment indicator, we will cover a series of processes which all relate to each other:

- staff selection
- induction of new employees
- appraisals.

Selecting effective staff

This process ranges from being quite important to really vital in the staffing of every organisation. It is very much related to the training and development potential of staff. People who are well suited to the job, who have the abilities and, especially in such areas as management, sales and marketing, the right personality, are likely to learn more quickly and effectively than those with no such aptitude. Testing for manual dexterity is also very useful in selecting employees who will be working, for example, in parts of the computer industry.

The process of selecting staff should take the form of:

- deciding on the objectives of the job
- carrying out a job analysis
- writing out a job description
- matching job skills to tests, especially psychometric tests.

The main types of psychometric tests are:

- aptitudes (especially work skills)
- ability (intelligence)
- achievement (skills already possessed)

- personality (you as you present yourself)

- interests (jobs which you like).

Such tests can be useful screening devices prior to interviewing and can be supplemented by 'realistic' processes such as:

- simulations
- group discussions
- in-tray exercises.

A mixture of these processes can take the form of an assessment centre which could take up part of a day, a whole day or several days depending on the nature and complexity of the job.

So for the identification of potential and possible lack of 'entry skills', tests can be of great value. Their effective use ensures that courses are not likely to involve a waste of money for new staff who do not have the necessary potential.

Induction

The process of induction is definitely regarded by IIP assessors as of great importance. It can supplement and quantify exactly the training needs identified during the selection process. Additionally, it can be very motivating to be orientated right at the beginning of your employment to the following aspects of the business:

- its **aims** and strategies

- its **products** and or services

- its **vision** of the future

- its general **culture**.

Induction makes a new employee feel that **they** are important to the organisation. It should be a productive and memorable process as well as having a practical outcome.

Applying HRD strategy to training

If you have a personnel or HRD strategy statement it can also be included in the part of your portfolio covering this indicator. If, for example, there is a specific policy for employees to take courses which the organisation, pays for and arranges, then the routine for doing this including the use of appropriate forms should also be documented in your IIP portfolio.

Appraising employees' development needs

This is an extremely important part of the Investors in People process. Some organisations use the term 'performance appraisal' because appraisals are about what employees will do, what they should learn, and is related to what they have already done.

Appraisals can provide portfolio evidence for no less than twelve of the 24 IIP indicators: 1.5, 2.2, 2.3, 2.4, 2.6, 3.2, 3.3, 3.4, 3.6, 4.1, 4.2 and 4.3. If you include training for managers in appraisal techniques, then indicators 2.5 and 3.5 could be added.

Making appraisals relevant

Why are appraisals so important in training and development? What are the aims of appraisal? To answer these questions you should relate the appraisal process to the business plan, *ie*:

- To improve organisational performance by reaching business goals.
- To improve team performance by achieving their organisational targets.
- To improve individual performance by reaching team goals.

Making appraisals constructive

The appraisal should be a **constructive discussion** of how the employee contributes to the organisation through carrying out his/her role effectively. It must relate to the appraisee's job description and training needs arising from it or from new skills (which should now be part of the job description). Training required could involve a small amount of instruction or coaching, followed by an assessment involving observation of performance. It could be the routine operation of a machine or computer-controlled device. It might be of a supervisor's skills in assessing at shop-floor level (TDLB Standards). It could be on the results obtained by a marketing or sales executive. As a manager, you could be appraised by your manager *and* by peers and subordinates, *ie* 360° appraisal.

Systematising appraisals

Since appraisals are usually the main way of establishing training needs, a detailed system must be planned. Directors and managers should set the overall policy and delegate managerial staff to draw up such a plan. They should start with objectives – decide on how *all* levels of staff will be appraised and by whom. Usually the best person for the job is the line manager. An informational paper should be devised which describes the system to all employees before it begins. Appraisers must then be trained so that they are credible, competent and seen to be impartial.

For detailed consideration of the process of appraising, see Chapter 10.

MANAGING DEVELOPMENT

2.4 Responsibility for developing people is clearly identified throughout the organisation, starting at the top.

Establishing responsibility

The chief executive or managing director is responsible for people development throughout the whole organisation. Normally, however, he/she would be responsible only for the training of the few very senior managers reporting direct to him/her (although much depends on the size of the organisation). Below this level the personnel or HRD department may well be responsible. Increasingly, however, identification of training needs lies with the **line manager** and to some extent to the team as a whole. If a group is inter-dependent then each member will have an excellent practical view of the others' training needs. The manager will be able hopefully to refer to the job description as to whether the individual has the main requirements of the skills of the job, checking these through actual performance.

Observing and identifying training needs

Whether by HRD or line manager, the usual method is by **observation** and **interview**. Additionally, precise needs can be perceived by:

- self-identification
- an observed gap in job capability
- matching to the standards of a VQ.

It is then up to the manager to work out with the individual what to do. Once the type of training has been decided on, along with where and when, the cost could be submitted for approval on an appropriate form with the written support of the line manager. Papers such as these can also be placed in the portfolio (section 2.4 and other relevant sections).

2.5 Managers are competent to carry out their responsibilities for developing people.

Establishing competences in training

What are the competences managers require? They should be able to:

- keep in mind the requirements of each person's job
- be able to identify training needs
- be aware of the training courses or processes required
- be able to go through effectively:
  (a) performance appraisal processes
  (b) less formal considerations of training
  short development plans – for ongoing personal and career development
- be able to coach, instruct and mentor when necessary
- evaluate training
- interpret results of training needs surveys in relation to their own departments
- provide equal opportunities.

Providing managerial training evidence

Training which is provided for managers in any of the above processes should be supported by evidence for the portfolio, for example:

- the programme of the course, in some detail
- examples of handouts

- evaluation forms in relation to the course
- certificates obtained by managers.

Since an important part of the assessment process for Investors in People is a programme of interviews of a sample of staff, it is important that managers should be able to discuss and answer questions on all aspects of their work with people.

SETTING TARGETS FOR TRAINING

2.6 Targets and standards are set for development actions.

What is meant by 'target' or 'standard'?

A target must be specific, *ie* an objective which is set in terms which are unmistakably precise (standards), for example: 'Will be able to operate [a specific machine] to a 99.5 per cent level of efficiency, producing [xxx] to a 99 per cent level of accuracy'.

As many employees now work towards training units or to complete VQs, this requirement is often quite easily met. VQs even include the idea of a defined standard because of their content of 'performance criteria' which are very specific. So if a target for an employee is to achieve a VQ or certain units of the VQ by a certain date, the requirements of IIP will be met.

If training does not involve a VQ then an objective can be set in the same kind of way, *ie* the specific process or knowledge must be acquired by a certain date as a result of training/instruction carried out in that particular way.

Timing target setting

Such targets can be set on such occasions as:

- the induction process
- the appraisal
- new aspect of a job about to start.

Relating targets to opportunities

Targets should always be noted on a performance appraisal form or personal development plan. Remember also that anyone, from chief executive to the newest employee, can identify their own targets as well as those set by appraisers. It is also the responsibility of the organisation to make all employees aware of training and development opportunities open to them.

LINKING TARGETS TO QUALIFICATIONS

> **2.7 Where appropriate, training targets are linked to achieving external standards, and particularly to National Vocational Qualifications (or relevant units) or Scottish Vocational Qualifications (SVQs).**

This assessment indicator does not require further elaboration except that employers and employees should be aware of VQs relevant to their jobs. As these are being quickly developed, more and more industries are becoming involved in setting their own standards. The Investors in People programme is very closely linked to National Training Targets as the target details in Figures 4 and 5 indicate.

Since the publication of the targets in Figure 4, 'Education and Training Targets for a competitive Scotland, Targets for 2000,' have restated the aims as shown in Figure 5.

Recognising IIP's importance

In both sets of targets, the percentage of organisations to be recognised or committed to Investors in People looks to be ambitious. In the Scottish wording 'learning' replaces 'training'. Training may produce learning but sometimes not – thus **learning** is really fundamental.

SUMMARY

- Every Investors in People Programme requires resources, especially a training budget, time off for essential training, people to do the training – either internal or external staff – and facilities such as training rooms and equipment.

- Training needs can be identified in terms of VQs. Line managers should know about relevant qualifications for their staff.

The National Education and Training Targets include:

- By 1996, 50 per cent of the workforce aiming for VQs or units towards them.
- By 2000, 50 per cent of the workforce qualified to at least NVQIII (or equivalent).
- By 1996, 50 per cent of medium to larger organisations to be Investors in People.
- By 1997, 80 per cent of young people to reach NVQII (or equivalent).
- Training and education to NVQIII (or equivalent) available to all young people who can benefit.
- By 2000, 50 per cent of young people to reach NVQIII (or equivalent).

Fig. 4. National education and training targets.

- Education and training leading to SVQ Level III/3 Highers (or equivalent) available to all young people who can benefit.
- By 1996 all employees should take part in training and development activities.
- By 1996 50 per cent of the workforce should be aiming for SVQs/NVQs or units towards them.

By the year 2000:

- 85 per cent of all young people to obtain SVQII/5 Standard Grades (or equivalent).
- 70 per cent of young people to obtain SVQ Level III/3 Highers (or equivalent).
- 60 per cent of the workforce to be qualified to at least SVQ Level III/3 Highers (or equivalent).
- 70 per cent of all organisations employing 200 or more employees, 35 per cent of those employing 50 or more, and 15 per cent of those employing under 50, to be recognised as Investors in People.

Fig. 5. Learning targets (Scotland).

- It is essential that training and development are related to the business plan, and such needs should be reviewed regularly.
- Reviews of training needs for individuals can occur during selection, induction and appraisal processes.
- Line managers require certain basic knowledge and skills so as to be able to appraise their staff.
- So that training can be evaluated, it is important that training targets should be set for individuals and teams.
- The people who have responsibility for training include directors, HRD staff and line managers.
- All developmental processes for individuals should be documented for the IIP portfolio.
- National training targets are quantified in terms of percentages of groups reaching VQ and other standards.
- Ambitious targets have been set for organisations to commit to or achieve IIP.

CASE STUDY

Ken wonders about bureaucracy

Ken Hills had been thinking about how he could reduce some of the Investors in People processes which a consultant had suggested as being important to develop.

'I just hate all these bureaucratic procedures', he complained to his deputy, Phil. 'Do we really have to organise such a complicated appraisal system for just twenty people? Couldn't we have monthly general staff meetings where everyone stands up and says what training or coaching they're having at the moment and what training they may need in future? One of us can write it down – or we could tape the whole session.'

'But they might not know what training they need', observed Phil.

'Generally speaking', argued Ken, 'most people do know what they need – or are told by colleagues. I don't think these formal appraisals will get us anywhere.'

'I don't agree', said Phil. 'Two people can work out what training is really needed better than an employee herself – and an appraiser will have a much better idea of which courses *are* available or who in the office has the skills needed to do coaching.'

'Another thing', said Ken, showing he had not been listening, 'couldn't we have one type of interview – if we do have to have them at all – covering personal development and appraisals and just have more of them – it would cut down a lot on paperwork. We wouldn't need to have to keep so many records.'

Flora, one of the managers who had joined the discussion, said, 'I don't see any objections to combining appraisals, PDPs and informal interviews as long as they are quite often, say every two to three months. And if I and Stuart are going to be the people who do the job we *must* keep to business objectives.'

'Okay', said Ken, 'but I think you should also speak about what our staff would *like* to do – even if it's not totally on business objectives.'

'Right, if you say so', said Phil, 'but these issues won't contribute to IIP. We must stick to job descriptions.'

'Do we actually have job descriptions now?' asked Ken.

'Oh yes', said the efficient Phil. 'I told you a couple of weeks ago we had finally managed to get them done.'

'Great, go ahead then', said Ken, 'I must dash off to a very important meeting – see you tomorrow!'

Question

Is there anything in Ken's view that IIP may be too bureaucratic and that individuals' personal preferences for training should be taken into account in making a decision?

DISCUSSION POINTS

1. Is it feasible to require that organisations must prove they are consistently willing to find necessary training before they can be recognised for IIP?

2. Do you think that giving employees time off to take courses is a bigger issue than providing funding for training?

3. Would career counselling contradict the IIP approach that training must be linked to the business plan of the organisation?

4. Before training is arranged for any individual or team, should that area of training have been agreed upon by the board and senior managers before an employee can be released or funded?

5. Do you think it would be a difficult process to identify and train the staff who would be most successful in carrying out appraisals and inductions? How would you set about it?

6
Achieving Investors in People: Actioning

As before, we start this chapter with the wording of the third principle, Action:

> *An Investor in People takes action to train and develop individuals on recruitment and throughout their employment.*
>
> Action should focus on the training needs of all new recruits and continually developing and improving the skills of existing employees.
>
> All employees should be encouraged to contribute to identifying and meeting their own job-related development needs.

INDUCTING NEW EMPLOYEES

> **3.1 All new employees are introduced effectively to the organisation and are given the training and development they need to do the job.**

Induction, being 'led in' to a new job, is for most people quite a difficult experience. It takes time to adjust to new people and new surroundings as well as a new job, or at least a new version of the same kind of job. Being promoted within the same organisation also requires new learning to take place and training can help avoid problems as well as produce bonuses. If it is a new job, then it is also the start of an important training and development process for the employee. Training needs must be identified and subsequent progress should be monitored during training and development interviews with the line manager when an ongoing PDP (personal development plan) can be started or updated.

Portfolio requirements

For Investors in People assessment you should have these processes working effectively and their documentation in the portfolio. For induction, these documents could include some or all of:

- the mission statement – the vision and aims of the occupation
- the business plan – and how it applies to your group
- the story of the organisation
- its main customers and their needs
- the various divisions, departments and sections
- the way its staff are deployed, *eg* teams, production groups
- the various sites of the organisation
- the group to which the new employee will be attached
- an organisation chart
- the specific job description: skills required and VQ equivalents
- health and safety policies
- terms and conditions of employment – including all policies, *eg* equal opportunities, training and development, career counselling, availability of stress counselling.

Mastering induction details

It would be of no value just to issue new staff with all the induction details and leave it to them to read through. This could be done when the staff are all 'professionals', but even then, some might just thumb their way through the text.

Using presentations

A better way of dealing with this for the majority of employees would be to have individual or group **presentations** by HRD staff or line managers, including a look at the documentation at the same time – with emphasis on studying the details further during interviews or team meetings. Of course the materials should be effectively presented with readable graphics, making the main points only.

Inductions must be **realistic**. If a totally unnatural picture of the organisation builds up the new employees' expectations too much, it may lead to absenteeism and early departure from the job, with resources having been wasted in training.

Phasing induction

It is a mistake to compress an induction procedure into one or two full days. To throw everything at a new employee in such a short time is inviting a mixed-up confusion of people, charts, factory areas and all sorts of details producing little or no relevant meaning. Inducting staff should also remember that the new employee has effectively three processes of induction:

- to the organisation as a whole
- to his/her team
- to his/her line manager.

Often the employee is very much aware of the line manager's way of working with his or her team but knows very little about the organisation as a whole. This is quite a serious lack because morale tends to relate to the organisation's reputation and atmosphere rather than to the team only.

So the induction process should be structured in such a way that the whole organisation is considered first, then the team and its role. Finally, the new employee will find out about the 'style' of the team leader. Finding out about the organisation and about his/her team role could well, for the employee, be spread out during one or two days per week over a period of three or four weeks, along with the practical experience of being supervised by the team leader.

DEVELOPING TARGETED SKILLS

> **3.2 The skills of existing employees are developed in line with business objectives.**

You should at this point in the book be well on the way to deciding for yourselves how to meet the requirements of this particular assessment indicator.

How can you ensure that training is directed towards **business objectives**?

The following are suggested as basic requirements:

- the line manager must be aware of business objectives
- he/she must know how their team contributes to meeting these objectives
- he/she must know which part of the employee's job description relates directly to business objectives
- the employee knows how his or her work helps towards meeting business objectives
- the line manager has identified training needs
- the employee is also aware of his/her training needs.

Complexity of jobs

All of the above situations are completely logical but we should remember that we are not always dealing with industrial type jobs or fairly simply described jobs. We are also dealing with all levels of staff working in areas like:

- micro-chip production
- computer programming
- sales
- marketing
- advertising
- recruitment
- design
- architecture
- computer-controlled factory production
- lecturing
- teaching
- local authority work
- administration
- education, including schools.

But it should not be too difficult to apply the basic induction information and processes to all types of work.

Opportunities for identifying training needs

The occasions when the skills required are identified, noted and training arranged and evaluated should also be considered. They might occur during:

- informal discussions
- personal development interviews
- appraisal interviews
- instruction/assessment sessions
- mentoring sessions.

Other situations where an existing employee may require training and/or development include the introduction of:

- new machinery
- new technology
- new product
- new types of course/qualifications

or the transfer of the employee to another department.

Connecting to the business plan

When new developments call for identification of training needs, it is not too difficult to explains **why** a course is taking place. At the same time, the new situation must reflect some part of the business plan, and this also should be explained. If notes or handouts are used, then the connection between the course and the business plan should be made clear even if it appears to be quite straightforward, *eg* this new development will help the company's profitability, increase cash flow, or expand opportunities for making profit. Again you should constantly keep in mind that such documents and course evaluation sheets should be kept for possible inclusion in the portfolio.

Other ways of familiarising all employees with news of such courses would be by:

- team meetings
- larger staff meetings
- company newsletters
- notice board information.

EXPLAINING TRAINING OPPORTUNITIES

> **3.3 All employees are made aware of the development opportunities open to them.**

A competent manager and a motivated employee will go out of their way to find out about such opportunities for both themselves and their teams. Remembering that **communication** is so important for IIP, the main forms of publicity are:

- through the appraisal/development interview system
- through team meetings and briefings
- company newsletter
- training bulletin
- official posters.

It is well known however that no matter how much you try, in the long run someone who should have seen these notices has not done so.

Publicising training

The fact is that simply publicising an opportunity is not enough. Many employees have to have these facts drawn to their attention. A really good team leader will do this – to describe and discuss relevant opportunities with individuals or team.

> House journals full of management propaganda are becoming a thing of the past.
>
> The more professional that company magazines become, the more challenges they are likely to face. The staff of Rover Group's house journal *Torque* discovered this when news came through of the takeover by BMW. . . . 'We had to withdraw the front page and produce an instant four page supplement to give staff all the news.'
>
> From 'It's good to talk with the staff', *Financial Mail on Sunday*, 5 November 1995.

ENCOURAGING EMPLOYEES

> **3.4 All employees are encouraged to help identify and meet their job/related needs.**

Some years ago, if a member of the sales staff had approached the personnel manager, waving enthusiastically a notice in the local newspaper about a course in creative selling, the manager would probably have been quite surprised at such initiative, even from sales.

With Investors in People, this kind of thinking should be encouraged. The day when a shop-floor employee looks up 'Occupations 96' in the Resources Centre for a VQ which will help develop his skills will indicate that he is working for an IIP organisation.

Using employee participation

As will be emphasised in this book, all training and development sessions should be **two-way**. The appraisee should be given plenty of opportunity to make suggestions about his/her training needs and ways of meeting them. The appraiser should describe and outline possible opportunities and help the appraisee come to a conclusion.

If the organisation has the initiative to conduct a training and development survey, employees should be empowered to suggest the kind of training they would like – going beyond the requirements of business-plan orientated training – and the methodology they would prefer, *eg* distance learning.

The essential point about assessment indicator 3.4 is that employees should learn to think they 'own' their training and development and that the better and more wide ranging it is, the better qualified they will be in the future.

MAKING IT WORK

> **3.5 Effective action takes place to achieve the training and development objectives of individuals and the organisation.**

'Effective' action means that the training agreed on during an appraisal/development interview really takes place and is successful. Only really skilled trainers, internal or external, should be employed and, after the course, the whole process should be **evaluated**, including the use of assessment sheets.

If effective training does not take place quickly:

- motivation diminishes
- the connection with the business plan is forgotten
- appraisals and development interviews are not taken seriously
- belief in a commitment to IIP is placed in doubt.

A system for action

After an appraisal, therefore, it is essential to have a **system** of taking things forward which should include some or all of the following:

- the appraiser is responsible for taking action
- he/she and the appraisee can complete a form requesting resources for training
- the appraiser should provide reasons and give support

- the request form is put forward to the appropriate staff member, *eg* personnel, HRD
- the result is reported to the line manager and the employee.

The main point is that action is taken regarding the required training.

INVOLVING MANAGERS

> **3.6 Managers are actively involved in supporting employees to meet their training and development needs.**

The most important phrase in this assessment criterion is 'actively involved in supporting'. 'Actively' suggests not just passive support but pressing for the required outcome. It may also appear to require 'support' before training only in terms of funding and time. In fact, support has to be provided **before, during** and **after** the actual training.

Before training there is the identification process of diagnosing need. At this stage also is, as discussed in 3.5, the process of obtaining approved funding, the portfolio evidence being an application document signed by a line manager, employee and HRD.

Essential information to be provided on an application form would be:

- name of employee
- job (job description attached)
- training needs
- course required
- reasons for course
- when
- how long
- cost

- travelling expenses
- manager's comments/support, signed by applicant, manager, HRD manager
- comments (for or against by senior manager/director), signed by senior manager/director.

During the process of training, the trainee and his/her line manager note its effectiveness or otherwise in terms of:

- increased skill
- increased speed.

The process of training is evaluated in an ongoing situation in terms of practicality, relevance, quantity and quality of feedback by trainers.

Portfolio evidence

Points such as these could be used as part of an evaluation of the course and could be used as a company feedback sheet. Similarly, the manager helps the trainee with practical on-the-job assessments, background theory and application of theory to practicalities. Active individual mentoring by the line manager can enhance the positive effect of the course and increase employee motivation.

Feedback on the actual course, however, is less important for the business than feedback on the employee's work full-time after returning to his/her job. The person who is best able to make such an evaluation is the employee's manager, who can see whether performance is better – in terms of quality, for example – than it was before. A report on the improvements should be placed in the space for 'manager's comments' on the same sheet as the employee has applied for the course. There could also be a comment space for the employee to be completed a week or two after returning to work. These records are vital in providing an IIP assessor with evidence for evaluation, *ie* were all the objectives as related to the business plan achieved by the employee?

SUMMARY

- An induction system is a necessary process for an organisation to achieve the Investors in People Standard. Although it is a very useful way of introducing employees to a new situation, it is also an introduction to the aims of the organisation and its business plan.

- Induction can also help in the process started during selection of identifying training needs. These needs will vary according to the employee's previous experience as well as his/her aptitudes and skills.

- Induction should be structured and phased so as to provide maximum understanding and application of information by the new employee.

- Training should be targeted against the skills required by the business plan and by the job description. Job descriptions should be amended when the job changes.

- Opportunities for employees learning new skills should not only be well publicised but brought to their notice as individuals. This should be the responsibility of the line manager and/or HRD.

- Training needs should be identified by the employee as well as by the line manager. Employees should be encouraged to describe their needs, not just in their present jobs but in preparation for promoted jobs which they might be able to apply for in the future.

- Once training and development needs have been identified, there must be a system which ensures that action takes place and that the objectives set are achieved.

- Managers should actively support employees in their applications for training, whether self diagnosed or suggested by the manager.

CASE STUDY

Ken identifies negative motivation

Ken Hill was just a little shaken. 'This really isn't on . . . I just don't believe it', he complained to his deputy Phil. 'He's only just started and now he's making trouble.'

'Oh, really, what happened?'

'Well, you know I was going to do an induction interview today with Bob Stevenson.'

'Yes.'

'Well, I thought it would be easy going, but now he's landed me with quite a problem.'

Then Ken went on to tell Phil of his woes. He had set aside a whole hour from his administrative duties and was going to complete Bob's induction. Bob had been briefed at the start of the week on how the organisation worked, who the staff were, what their roles were, and where they were based in the building. He had been informed of the business plan, had read thoroughly the mission statement, and had gone out on visits with all 'outside' staff. He had even been told about all the office stationery, reference books, technology systems (with a promise of training) – in fact, everything he needed to know.

'When we started the meeting everything was fine', observed Ken. 'I was writing down various particulars about training on his PDP and then we came to that course that all the business start-up advisers are going to attend.'

'Oh yes', said Phil, 'where the new arrangements with the TEC for people wanting to apply for business start-up grants, all the new forms, interviews with banks, possible sponsorships would all be considered.'

'Exactly', said Ken, 'and would you agree that it is very relevant to the job?'

'Absolutely', exclaimed Phil, 'no one could know the ropes over the next few months without going to the course, getting the handouts and reading them up.'

'Well', said Ken, 'Bob's refused to go.'

'Refused!' exclaimed Phil. 'That's impossible, especially as he's just started and should be totally enthusiastic. Why on earth has he refused?'

'Well, all he said was "It's not in my job description".'

'And isn't it?' asked Phil.

'No, of course not. I've always assumed that we were so friendly and positive here that we would have staff who would be delighted to have this kind of extra help. All I can assume is that Bob has such a large ego that he thinks he doesn't need to learn any more.'

'What can we do?' said Phil. 'Try to persuade him to go?'

'I don't think that will work', said Ken. 'He'd just come back at me aggressively. Do you know what he said?'

'Go on', said Phil.

'He said, "Are you trying to tell me I don't know how to set up a business after 40 years' experience?"'

'Well, I can see that, but surely he must know that there will always be changes in detail', observed Phil. 'But, wait a minute, I have an idea.'

'What's that?' asked Ken.

'Isn't it just possible that he doesn't think he'll be able to cope with these new ideas?'

'I can hardly believe that', said Ken, 'but . . . I did mention to him that attending the course and doing the work might help him to achieve a course certificate . . . which might mean someone observing him and giving him some kind of assessment.

'So instead of threatening not to renew his contract, which was on my mind, I feel we should be giving him more confidence rather than assuming he has over much of it. We know that he is exceptionally able – let's try to build on this policy and see how it goes.'

Question

Do you agree that often it is a good idea to look more closely into negative behaviour than just the most obvious reasons? Is fear often concealed behind an irrelevant reason?

DISCUSSION POINTS

1. Do you think that all levels of staff should have an induction into the business, including even non-executive directors?

2. To what extent should employees at the same level as the inductee be involved in his/her induction?

3. What could be the motivation for:
   (a) employees identifying their own training needs
   (b) managers actively supporting employees' requests for training and development?

4. What kind of information should you be seeking when evaluating induction processes?

5. Should you ideally embark on induction with one group of employees, a sample of employees or all employees?

7
Achieving Investors in People: Evaluation

This chapter on evaluation deals with an IIP area which has often caused difficulties for participating organisations. Why? Because it is a concept which has not been used on a large scale in business for very long. Yet it is really very simple. It means 'to find or judge value'. So you should ask yourself 'Have our training and development programmes been successful: what has been their value?'

If you have a business plan including specific, measurable objectives, you can assess the impact of training on the business programme, *ie* you evaluate. In doing so you can, by checking on what has happened, improve, if necessary, on what will happen.

At this point, you are reminded of the heading of the fourth IIP principle: evaluation.

> *An Investor in People evaluates the investment in training and development to assess achievement and improve future effectiveness.*
>
> The investment, the competence and commitment of employees, and the use made of skills learned should be reviewed at all levels against business goals and targets.
>
> The effectiveness of training and development should be reviewed at the top level and lead to renewed commitment and target setting.

EVALUATING PROGRESS

> **4.1 The organisation evaluates how its development of people is contributing to business goals and targets.**

The main way in which an organisation can evaluate and monitor continuously the extent to which people development is helping to progress business goals is by assessing how far along the line the business is towards reaching its objectives.

Justifying evaluation

Note that training and development is not now seen as a liability or expense with no obvious pay-off, but as an **investment**. The next step is to ask 'To what extent has it worked?' The next question could be 'How much better will we be able to perform once the improvements pointed to by evaluation have taken effect?' So you are also evaluating **quality** and **value**.

First steps

First, you go back to the details of your business plan, take each objective and measure progress by the following type of assessment indicators:

- production
- turnover
- savings
- quality
- time
- returned goods rate
- re-working.

Setting performance targets

If you have set goals with measurable targets, *eg* 25 per cent increase in **production**, **turnover** or **savings**, you can readily check on this. Supposing each of these targets has moved 15 per cent, 10 per cent and 7 per cent respectively towards its goal and this programme has been paralleled by and equated to systematic job-related training, then the overall statistics look promising, especially if the targets have been set quite recently. If objectives can be split into targets for the teams and even individuals and they also can be monitored for progress, so much the better for motivation through accurate feedback.

Consideration of such results should be a matter for senior management who, in turn, can adjust strategies to improve performance if necessary and also continue to commit themselves to IIP. Again, the minutes of such meetings should be available for the IIP portfolio.

4.2 The organisation evaluates whether its development actions have achieved their objectives.

You might think that this assessment indicator is the same as 4.1 but you have probably noticed that it uses the term 'achieved' as opposed to 'contributing to'. With 4.1, if the process of development and improvements go hand in hand, it is reasonable to suggest that the first is at the very least having some effect on the second.

An important feature of this type of evaluation is that there must be targets and time limits in the business plan. If a timescale for reaching the targets described in 4.1 had been twelve months and the interim figures referred to progress made in six months only, there would be total certainty that the progress made had been extremely satisfactory. The latter would be **ongoing** or **formative** evaluation, whilst the one year consolidation would be **summative**.

EVALUATING CHANGE

Investors in People can be regarded as part of a total quality management (TQM) programme, the basic aim being the process of continuous improvement. Again, the criteria will be such measures as production, quality and waste reduction. Quality could include meeting the demands of customers efficiently with criteria such as improved customers' ratings or reduced numbers of complaints.

In many organisations, the starting point for evaluation will have been the commencement of a TQM programme or Investors in People.

Measuring change processes

Suppose, however, you wanted to find out if Investors in People had resulted in real improvements when compared with the period prior to its introduction. In theory, you could use an experimental approach in which an IIP group's performance was compared with a control group, where everything would remain as before over the same period of time and using the same criteria. But this would be very difficult, especially in terms of controlling other variables, *eg* quality of management.

Another much easier way would be to start measuring against assessment indicators before the onset of the IIP programme and then continuously monitor after its commencement. Again variables such as production levels would tend to vary according to customer demand and the economic climate. But one would normally be looking for improvements in performance from the IIP starting point, initially at quite a small level, but increasing as the programme accelerated.

Yet another indicator would be performance as benchmarked against competitors. If your organisation improves by a five per cent factor in productivity, it will be less satisfying if your main competitor over the same period has accelerated by ten per cent. This therefore is another factor in setting targets.

EVALUATING AT ALL LEVELS

4.3 The outcomes of training and development are evaluated at individual, team and organisational levels.

We shall take each of these levels in turn:

- individual
- team
- organisation.

Evaluating individual performance

How an individual gains from the learning process during training can, as we have seen, be self assessed by the employee or more objectively by his/her performance on the job by the team leader or line manager. Ideally, they will have, prior to training, agreed on objectives and targets during the appraisal. These objectives or action points will have been listed on the appraisal document.

How can performance on the job be evaluated? Some ways of doing this are by using one or more of the following:

- pre and post tests (of performance and knowledge)
- observation of performance (by manager)
- written tests (underpinning knowledge)
- practical tests (manager)

- post-training questionnaire (attitudes towards course efficiency interest) (see Figure 6).

	Very well	*Fairly well*	*Not well*	*Comments*
1. Were you aware of why you were attending this course?				
2. Did you know the objectives of the course?				
3. Did the course teach you to master the essential skills?				
4. Were the teaching methods effective?				
5. Did the instructors motivate you?				
6. Did the instructors show they knew about the company business plan?				
7. Did the instructors relate the training to the business plan?				

Fig. 6. Example of a post-training questionnaire.

The evaluation process can cover all the different types of training – courses of various lengths, VQs, projects and work shadowing. Records of ongoing individual targets and projects with results and evaluations should also be kept in the individual's personal development plan documentation.

Evaluating team performance

Team training objectives will have been set by the team leader/manager in conjunction with senior management's plans and strategies. The leader will then be committed to these targets in measurable terms or units within a particular time limit. The best leaders will be able to do this having talked to the team and reached agreed objectives with them.

As with the individual and the business as a whole, teams benefit from **feedback** on progress towards objectives. Team motivation will be increased by rapid, positive feedback. This information could be provided by the team leader during briefings or by feedback checklists showing targets achieved. Team meetings can also be used to provide group feedback information from management on how the team's performance has helped reach business goals. Results on VQ assessment performance or on MCI (Management Charter Initiative) achievements can be announced in the same way.

Evaluating team role competences

Teams can, of course, operate at different levels – shop-floor employees, product management teams, HR teams, sales and marketing and inter-group. They do not always have to be involved in 'traditional areas'. Empowered groups, as well as being involved in specific jobs, can also be involved in problem solving roles such as quality and JIT (just-in-time) approaches. This may need training in problem solving and each may have a role in which they could benefit from coaching.

Some may require coaching or training in managerial competences such as:

- setting objectives
- conducting meetings
- planning
- decision making
- assessing
- communicating.

Team leaders can also study course evaluation sheets completed by individuals within their team and, in turn, complete a questionnaire (see Figure 7) which will help to systematise their reports to senior managers on changes in team performance.

To be completed by managers after team course/training has been completed and they have studied evaluation responses and assessed employees' work skills

What were the objectives of the training?

How much did the team learn?	All competences	Some	Few
How much underpinning knowledge was gained?	All main points	Some main points	Few main points
What percentages of improvements have been achieved in:- output – quality –			
Generally have the objectives been achieved?		Yes	No
Were connections to the business plan understood?		Yes	No
Will further support training be required?		Yes	No

Fig. 7. Evaluating team training experiences.

EVALUATING AT SENIOR LEVEL

Evaluating organisational performance

To achieve a picture of the performance of a whole organisation could be quite a complex process, but every effort should be made to keep it as **simple** as possible.

Top management can combine information from divisions, groups and teams in relation to each of the objectives of the business plan. Additionally, the extent to which each such group has contributed to the plan can be assessed from comparing their actual performances with the targets set for them. Training and development effects can also be assessed by company performance statistics with the equivalent statistics prior to the IIP programme when there was probably no systematic parallel training to the specific aims of the plan.

The top management team can also study the results of employee surveys with the steps they have taken to provide training opportunities to the perceived needs of the employees of the whole organisation. They use exactly the same approach as the line manager and team leader.

The process represents a big increase in **inter-communication** which, in turn, calls for a considerable effort to produce accurate basic information up the line which, in turn, is fed back to the whole organisation.

Information keeping and evaluation

Keeping a record of basic informational statistics and of many meetings at all levels and then selecting an illustrative sample for IIP purposes will be an invaluable part of your portfolio. Any evidence which shows a series of interconnected steps is particularly effective. It is the decisive step in the cycle of identifying training needs against the business plan, providing action in the form of training and development and then evaluating results. Previously, organisations had often assumed that training was sure to have an effect. Now this is not acceptable. Improvement must be made evident and evaluation is the part of the feedback loop which enables continuous organisational improvement. We may expect the most effective training to be evidenced by actual results. If these are not satisfactory, faults must be identified and put right through better training processes.

At this point we can sum up by noting that the processes on which evaluation is built are:

- information keeping
- details of objectives
- how achievement of objectives is measured
- ongoing monitoring at all levels
- summative reviews.

Evaluating attitudinal effects

It is necessary in evaluating training and development to give a recognised place to what are sometimes called 'affective' components, *ie* changes in attitude. Some attitudes invariably have an emotional as well as a cognitive (intellectual) component. Attitudes too can often have more effect on performance than purely logical/mechanical learning. If training is seen as helping individual as well as organisation survival, then it becomes a positive motivational process in itself. In addition, team spirit and positive outlook can produce the competitive edge which is so necessary for the continuing change processes in organisations.

One way of assessing affective outcomes is by way of relevant items in an organisational questionnaire. This could contain questions like:

Having completed this course do you feel more positive now about achieving:

- your own action plan's objectives
- the team's performance objectives
- the organisation's targets as in the business plan?

Positive responses to questions such as these can provide a measure of contemporary organisational **morale**. Information of this kind can equally be included in the Investors in People portfolio.

4.4 Top management understands the broad costs and benefits of developing people.

Evidence of top management's understanding of costs is most effectively illustrated by the existence of a ring-fenced comprehensive training budget which has been based on realistic consideration of planned training needs.

A training budget has to take into consideration:

- payment of course fees including certificates at all levels
- expenses of running internal courses, *eg* development centres organised by external tutors or by internal staff
- travel and accommodation costs for individuals and teams
- time cost – training time for employees who are therefore not doing their normal work.

Evidence for these costs for fees and time can be provided in the portfolio, but the main requirement is for the existence of a training budget.

As to **benefits**, the most cogent understanding of them comes from concrete evidence of increased business and better quality represented

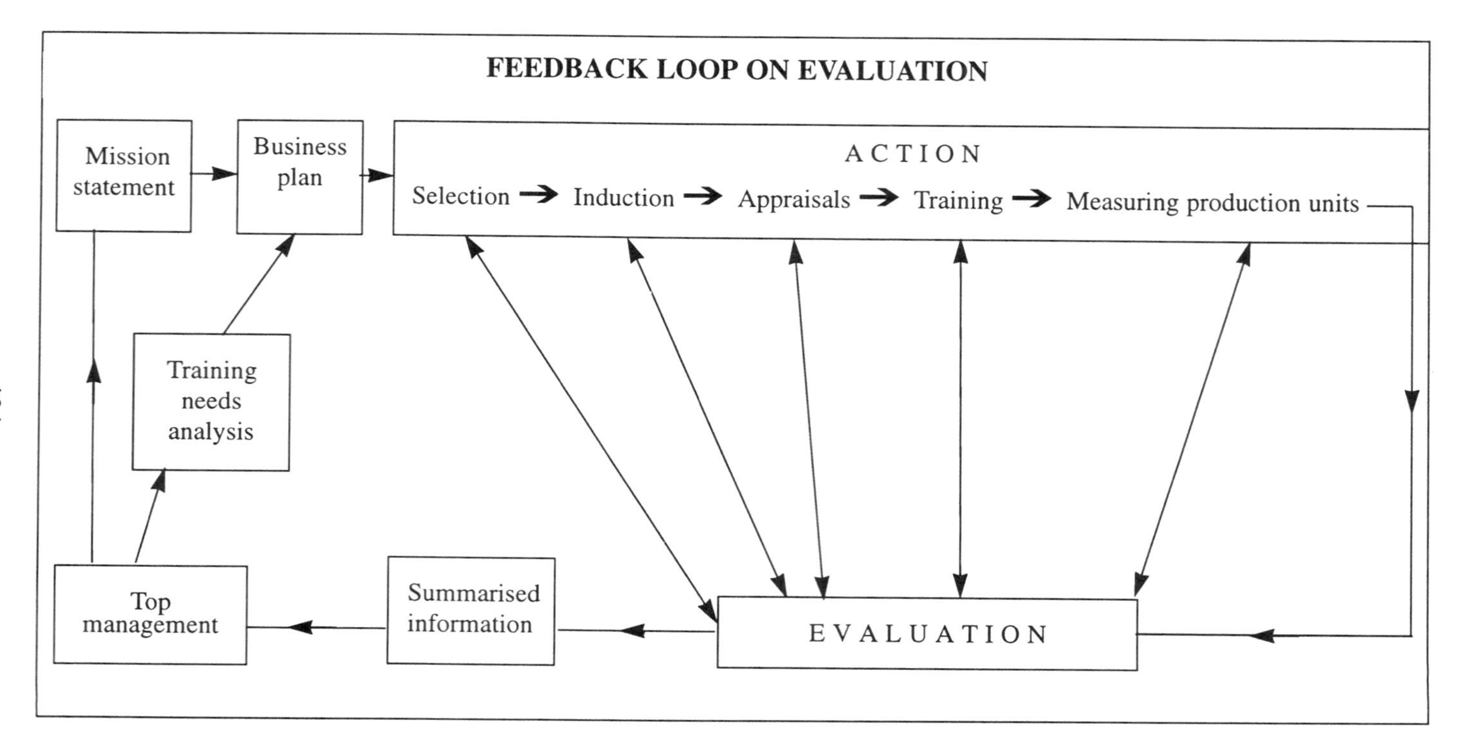

Fig. 8. Feedback loop on evaluation.

by customer surveys, interviews and positive evaluations. Do increased productivity and profits, for example, reflect the objectives of the business plan? If so, the strategy developed from the plan, including IIP, has produced added value to outgoings. Of course, this may not always happen in every detail. Some training may not pay its way or produce better service. But it is always better to know this than to be unaware. Amount and type of training can be varied according to results. If every section of an organisation uniformly shows the benefits, then top management should be thoroughly convinced of the value of IIP.

Evidence for the portfolio reflecting indicator 4.4 would therefore be:

- details of the training budget
- details of time costs
- course descriptions and evaluations
- reports from line managers and team leaders
- statistics on profit, turnover, productivity sales and quality.

Mapping the evaluation process

From what we have seen so far about evaluation, it emerges that it is part of a feedback loop system (see Figure 8).

The action processes of selecting, inducting and training staff are equated to production units (or other forms of measurement) and evaluated in line with progress towards the targets of the business plan. Feedback relates to the effectiveness of each of the different parts of the action process.

Information from managers and team leaders is consolidated in a report on progress for top management. Then the HRD department or its equivalent carry out an organisation-wide training needs analysis. The evaluation information might also be supplemented by a survey of training needs completed by every employee. Results are conveyed to top management, who can then modify the business plan.

SHOWING COMMITMENT

4.5 The continuing commitment of top management to developing people is communicated to all employees.

This indicator can relate to two different phases:

- during the period from commitment to achievement of IIP
- after achieving the IIP Standard and keeping to it for the three year period before reassessment – referred to sometimes as a phase of **maintenance evaluation**.

Both of these situations can be covered through the processes of communication:

- Top management continue to support induction, appraisal, training and development actions and evaluation.
- They continue to provide a training budget.
- The IIP representative group of staff are encouraged to attend local network groups arranged by TECs and LECs. Involvement like this shows the positive attitude of the organisation, especially if such meetings occur in their own premises periodically.
- At large meetings – where as many staff as possible attend – continuing commitment is re-iterated. Often, at such meetings, smaller groups can, as part of the programme, discuss aspects of the IIP Standard and report back. Discussion on 'Are we as an organisation ready for IIP assessment?' can be enlightening. Top managers can be actively involved in these sub group meetings and get to know grass root levels of awareness.

Equally important are the usual channels – newsletters and company newspapers, notice boards and periodic news sheets on IIP only where enthusiasm and commitment are expressed by:

- news of individuals and teams gaining qualifications
- videos and photographs of presentations of certificates
- reports of team successes in production and sales
- reports of employee surveys of training and development needs

- new initiatives with relevant training programmes.

Again it should be stressed that all possible documentation arising from these activities should be stored and kept available for the portfolio:

- minutes and descriptions of internal meetings and networks
- copies of newsletters, noticeboard posters, videos of meetings and presentations.

Finally, an ongoing organisational pledge to the IIP Standard could be conveyed in many of these types of communication.

SUMMARY

- Use the business plan to evaluate continuing progress.
- Specific objectives enable the organisation to assess how much progress it has made towards them in a particular timescale.
- Criteria such as production, turnover, profit and re-working should be identified and quantified. Benchmarking can also be employed.
- Objectives can be set for individuals, teams and the organisation – and results evaluated.
- Targets and objectives can be ongoing and summative.
- Evaluations can also be made of the effects of courses as well as through questionnaires seeking opinions on interest and usefulness.
- Top management can evaluate training in relation to its cumulative effects on the achievement of company goals.
- Using an organisational questionnaire to assess attitudes can indicate the effects of positive or negative morale.
- Top management can equate improvements in company performance from their investment (monetary) in training and development.

- Top management should convey their continued commitment to Investors in People through all the most effective communication channels. They should take part personally in this.

- A feedback loop diagram illustrates the evaluative process.

CASE STUDY

Co-operating on evaluation

Vernon and Ryan were beginning to work together after six months of adopting a policy of achieving Investors in People. Vernon had regained much of his enthusiasm although he was still sceptical of the objectives/targets management approach. Ryan also saw that Vernon had some good ideas and had real practical experience behind him which could be applied successfully for 'fire fighting' purposes.

The chief executive, James Goodlad, and Vernon's colleagues in senior management were very pleased with progress, especially in the development of an appraisal system. However, one important step which still had to be taken, and which shows how PACTEC were now out-of-date, was to reorganise into a system of self-managing teams, each with a team leader.

Vernon and Ryan had been entrusted to see this process through. They had already carried through the vital steps of identifying the roles and objectives of the new team leaders and on the basis of a job analysis had written out a job description. Team leaders had been selected. Now they, Vernon and Ryan, had to plan out a training process for them.

'I'll look out a plan for defining training needs which fits in well with IIP and which I found in a management book', promised Ryan, when they were discussing how to organise the training.

'Well, don't forget', said Vernon, 'I want to see that later today or tomorrow at the latest.'

'Tomorrow', said Ryan, playing for time, and indeed he did appear the next day with some papers.

'I think this will do', he said, unfolding a sheet on Vernon's flipchart (without asking).

'We start off with headings like this. Let's try to complete the table.'

Figure 9 was the result of their deliberations.

When they had completed the table Vernon and Ryan looked at each other with self-congratulatory pleasure.

'Looks OK', said Vernon. 'It seems to have everything in it we need, including measurement for evaluation purposes.'

'It's not just OK!', exclaimed Ryan. 'It's absolutely brilliant!'

Business plan objectives	Greater productivity
Sub objective	Reorganise into self-managing teams
Learning required	Team leadership Team selection Team building Team roles
Training	Effective leadership styles Selection techniques Simulations Belbin's roles for managers and team leaders
Measurement of productivity	Units manufactured % decrease in returned units % increase in certificates of quality from customers

Fig. 9. Defining training needs.

Question

How would the plan agreed between Vernon and Ryan help to evaluate the effects of training on team leaders?

DISCUSSION POINTS

1. Why do you think that training and development were until recently rarely evaluated?

2. List all the different factors in your work sector which could be used as indicators for purposes of evaluating training.

3. What are the reasons why evaluating organisational change is particularly difficult?

4. Write down six convincing reasons on why the evaluation of training and development is really essential in business.

8
Compiling a Portfolio

In putting together a portfolio of evidence (a collection of papers and other materials such as videos), you are proving to the assessor that your organisation carries out all the activities relating to the four IIP principles and 24 indicators. It need not be an extremely large collection, especially for smaller organisations where written documentation will not exist to the same extent in the first place. Increasing emphasis is being placed on *verbal* evidence but a certain amount of documentation can be very useful to an assessor. Much depends on factors such as the size and type of business involved.

Why is a portfolio needed?

Your portfolio is **essential** for the assessment process because it lets the assessor actually see the primary evidence, which is the documentation in the portfolio supporting your claim to be an Investor in People.

Although it is part of the assessment evidence and is hopefully the final step in your IIP process, you should start putting it together from the **early stages** of your programme. At the start, you do not need to be very selective. It could be as simple a process, especially in a small organisation, of putting every possible paper which might be relevant into a box file.

How the Assessor obtains evidence

Two types of evidence are inspected by the assessor:

1. **Primary** – documentation in the portfolio
2. **Secondary** – evidence from interviews with a sample of staff, ranging from the most senior to the most junior. The assessor will note the main points given in response to his/her questions or during general discussion with staff.

The main reason for secondary evidence is that possibly not all of the assessment indicators have been covered by primary evidence and question/answer/discussion evidence can fill any gaps. Other reasons are that it confirms that what is described in the primary evidence of the portfolio (*eg* inductions) really does happen and that the same processes exist on the other sites of larger organisations.

Selecting documents

In choosing relevant documents, remember the following points:

- documents should reflect activities and processes which have been in place for some time and are working efficiently
- documents should also be up-to-date, *eg* revised recently
- documents should provide evidence for an indicator or indicators
- it should be quite clear which indicator document they support.

COLLECTING THE EVIDENCE

As with all aspects of Investors in People, it is always an advantage to give a staff member responsibility for a specific task. Someone is definitely needed to organise the portfolio. It could be the chairperson of the IIP working group or a member of the group. Yet again it could be someone not involved so far. The IIP group chairperson is probably very busy already, and a 'newcomer' may have to learn a great deal about IIP before starting, so the ideal person would be an **existing group member**. You are also looking for someone who has a good knowledge of the papers circulating in the organisation and which are used a great deal and who is also neat, tidy and methodical.

The job involves:

- gathering all possible relevant papers
- matching these to assessment indicators
- keeping papers not yet categorised in secure storage.

First steps in categorising

To start categorising papers, you could group them roughly into the four overall areas of principles – commitment, review, action, evaluation – and then allocate through each of them from your stored papers.

This categorisation could include:

Commitment
Letters of commitment to the chief executive of TEC/LEC and reply, the business plan or extracts, headed by the mission statement and statement of the organisation's ambitions. Training strategies relating to the plan must also be included. It could also include a newsletter giving facts about IIP to the workforce.

Review
This section could include materials on how managers plan training with employees, training budgets, who is responsible for training, appraisal interviews and the ways in which action on agreed training is taken.

Action
Here you would include papers on an induction system and on any training provided for managers in induction processes and appraisals.

Evaluation
Relevant papers here would be on:

- the objectives of training

- pre-training sessions with the team leader or manager about the objectives of training

- post-training meetings with the team lead on effects.

Other important evidence would be completed evaluation sheets on specific courses, and the minutes of senior managers' meetings during which the overall effects of training on achieving the business plan have been evaluated. Remember that the papers suggested are examples and that you should use your initiative and creativity within your own situation.

DESIGNING THE FRAMEWORK

So far we have covered the design of a stepped programme and framework:

- collect and store all documents which could be relevant
- select papers relevant to the four principles of IIP.

Your next two steps are:

- design your portfolio grid
- re-allocate papers to each of the headings in your portfolio.

Re-categorising material

This process is one of defining evidence into more and more specialised sub headings. You may finally arrive at headings such as these:

File heading

(A) Organisational chart – showing the range of jobs with names of employees.

(B) Letter of commitment to TEC/LEC and reply.
Certificate of Commitment. Action plan.

(C) Mission statement and business plan, including associated training and development needs.

(D) Training and strategy papers; HRD policy/strategy statement.

(E) Training budget. An analysis of costs including time.

(F) Survey of staff training forms – completed. Evaluation of information from staff survey.
Evaluation forms – for staff to complete after a course of training.
Summary form for team leaders/managers on effects of training on their groups.
Minutes of directors' meetings evaluating the effects of training on the organisation's strategy.

(G) Staff induction (sample of papers including an individual's programme and completed personal development plan showing training needs and actions).

(H) Appraisal forms – for different staff levels – completed quite recently.
Papers on managerial training for carrying out appraisals, *eg* content of course and methodology.

(I) Copies of individual training plans and/or personal development plans.

(J) Minutes of management/union meetings relating to training, development and Investors in People.

Note that the above headings are examples only of what you can include. Another heading could be Job Descriptions.

Numbering documents

Where there are several different types of written material in one category, they should then be numbered; so, if there were four pieces of evidence in file section E, they should be numbered E1, E2, E3, E4 and

File	Evidence		Commitment						Review							Action						Evaluation				
			1.1	1.2	1.3	1.4	1.5	1.6	2.1	2.2	2.3	2.4	2.5	2.6	2.7	3.1	3.2	3.3	3.4	3.5	3.6	4.1	4.2	4.3	4.4	4.5
A	Organisational chart		✓				✓					✓														
B	Action plan	(1)	✓				✓	✓								✓						✓				
	Letter of commitment	(2)	✓					✓																		
	Reply to letter of commitment	(3)	✓					✓																		
	Certificate of Commitment	(4)	✓			✓																				
C	Mission statement	(1)	✓	✓				✓																		✓
	Business plan	(2)	✓	✓	✓	✓		✓	✓			✓		✓	✓										✓	✓
D	Training and strategy papers	(1)	✓		✓	✓		✓	✓			✓			✓			✓								
	HRD policy statement	(2)	✓		✓	✓			✓			✓						✓								
E	Training budget	(1)	✓		✓				✓																	
	Analysis of costs	(2)							✓															✓	✓	
F	Survey of staff training needs	(1)		✓				✓		✓	✓		✓				✓		✓			✓	✓	✓		
	Evaluation forms	(2)																				✓	✓	✓		
G	Staff induction forms	(1)																								
	Personal development plans	(2)					✓				✓			✓		✓		✓	✓							
H	Appraisal forms	(1)					✓			✓	✓	✓		✓			✓	✓	✓		✓	✓	✓	✓		
	Appraisal training	(2)					✓			✓	✓	✓	✓	✓			✓	✓	✓	✓	✓	✓	✓	✓		

Fig. 10. Example of an IIP portfolio matrix.

indexed accordingly. (Remember that forms which have been completed are more effective than blank forms, but, of course confidentiality must be maintained. It would be possible for names to be temporarily covered over while being looked at by the assessor.)

Training records

Employee files usually contain two types of information – **personal**, which does not need to be looked at by an assessor, and **training records** including appraisals which could be available for an assessor to see. It is often an advantage for employees to have a copy themselves of their training records so they are aware of what they have achieved and what they still have to do, *eg* moving a VQ level up from where they are at the moment. It also helps if they are being interviewed by an IIP assessor where they can update themselves quickly.

USING A MATRIX REFERENCE SYSTEM

This system is commonly used as part of the portfolio gathering of evidence procedure.

It takes the form of a table where the assessment indicator numbers are on the horizontal axis and the storage folder index of categories on the vertical (see Figure 10). This system can act as:

- a check for you to see that each indicator is covered – preferably by three pieces of information
- a check for the assessor to see if he or she needs additional secondary evidence
- a help for assessors to see exactly what evidence is available and where they can find it.

EDITING RELEVANT EVIDENCE

Although you should gather as much evidence as you can for the portfolio, it is important to remember that you should not have too much. One hears stories – probably false – of assessors being shown into rooms with a large number of filing cabinets. The IIP organisers wave their hands in the direction of the cabinets saying 'There's our evidence – feel free to look at any of the papers.'

Every paper you provide should be really **essential**. Check each one to ensure that it provides evidence which is required and which does not overlap to any extent with any other paper. Papers which cover several indicators are particularly useful.

Making fine judgements

Sometimes decisions can deal with borderline instances. Supposing that your organisation's business plan contains an appendix dealing with staff training and development which goes into very great detail. On the other hand, there is a summary paper which covers all the main areas relating to needs developing from the plan. You should almost certainly use the shorter paper.

Support material

But the longer paper might just be needed by the assessor. What you would do is to have a standby collection of papers which have been difficult to categorise as totally essential. This extra file could be kept beside the main portfolio, but it might be able to add invaluable evidence which the assessor required. Remember, however, that the only **absolutely essential** papers are the written but flexible business plan, which sets out targets and goals, and a paper identifying the broad development needs associated with the plan and how these will be assessed and met.

SUMMARY

- The two types of portfolio evidence.
- How to select relevant documents.
- Delegating the task.
- Examples of relevant documents relating to the assessment indicators.
- Designing a framework for collecting, categorising and storing documents.
- Cross-referencing portfolio material with the indicators.
- Editing evidence – in and out.
- Examples of portfolio evidence for all the assessment indicators.

CASE STUDY

Mary's hard work pays off

'How on earth do we know what to put in the portfolio?' asked the agitated Alex Thomson-Bell. 'Shall we put every single thing that has the remotest connection with IIP in and hope for the best?'

'No', replied Mary Hughes, one of her senior assistants, as respectfully as she could, 'we have been warned you know that that kind of approach can give the assessor three times as much work as they need to do and increases the costs of our assessment.'

'Oh, right! Could you do this then? I'm up to the eyes on the Harrogate contract and I can't be late with that one. And, oh, here are some IIP papers that have been on my desk for weeks . . . please have a look at them.'

Mary picked them up and, although she was also very busy, probably busier than Alex, she decided to 'crack' the IIP portfolio problem.

Fortunately, as she looked through the papers, she came across the suggested ways of using a table (matrix) with evidence headings on the vertical dimension and the IIP indicators on the horizontal.

Using the same approach, even with papers which she immediately remembered about, she soon thought of about eight headings. The suggestion that videos could be included set her to writing in 'Induction video' (a recently completed project by some of her colleagues at AT-B).

Now she decided she would adopt a new tack – write down each of the indicators and opposite each one, from the already collected papers, write down which of them covered the indicators.

This is the pattern developed:

	Indicator	Portfolio evidence
1.1	There is a public commitment from the most senior level within the organisation to develop people.	Letter of commitment and mission statement.
1.2	Employees at all levels are aware of the broad aims or vision of the organisation.	Mission statement. General and team level meetings – minutes. Newsletters.
1.3	There is a written but flexible plan which sets out business goals and targets.	Business plan or extracts.
1.4	The plan identifies broad development needs	Business plan or extracts.

	and specifies how they will be assessed and met.	Details of VQs to be achieved.
1.5	The employer has considered what employees at all levels will contribute to the success of the organisation and has communicated this effectively to them.	Mission statement. Personal development plans. Team meetings and briefings – minutes or written accounts. Questionnaire for surveys and results of surveys.
1.6	Where representative structures exist, management communicates with employee representatives a vision of where the organisation is going and the contributions employees (and their representatives) will make to its success.	Minutes of joint meetings where mission statement, business plan *etc* discussed positively and strategies agreed.
2.1	The written plan identifies the resources that will be used to meet training and development need.	Business plan – section on resources required. Training budget – copy.
2.2	Training and development needs are regularly reviewed against business objectives.	Appraisal system – papers. Survey of training needs – results. Meetings of directors/top management on this subject. Information and statistics from team leaders. ISO9000 manual.
2.3	A process exists for regularly reviewing the training and development needs of all employees.	Appraisals – examples. Personal development plans – updated records from line managers.
2.4	Responsibility for developing people is clearly identified throughout the organisation, starting at the top.	Organisational chart. Job descriptions. Mentoring/instructional activities – statements/ checklists – signed by managers.
2.5	Managers are competent to carry out their	Course descriptions on

	responsibilities for developing people.	appraising, training, and assessing. Certificates achieved in the process (VQs, MCI).
2.6	Targets and standards are set for development.	Objectives agreed at appraisals or development interviews – documents. VQ, MCI certificates. Organisation's safety plan. Team targets – minutes of meeting.
2.7	Where appropriate training targets are linked to achieving external standards, and particularly to National Vocational Qualifications or (Scottish locational qualifications in Scotland) and units.	Appraisals – objectives. Use of NVQ/SVQ/MCI units. Copies of any certificates. ISO9000 accreditation.
3.1	All new employees are introduced effectively to the organisation and are given the training and development they need to do their jobs.	Induction procedures – documentation and video. Personal development and/or training plans. NVQ/SVQ certificates. Induction evaluation forms completed.
3.2	The skills of existing employees are developed in line with business objectives.	Individual and team training plans. Course descriptions. Evaluation information for line managers. Directors/top management discussions – minutes.
3.3	All employees are made aware of the development opportunities open to them.	Meetings of teams, groups, – minutes. Newsletters – notice-boards examples.
3.4	All employees are encouraged to help identify and meet their job-related development needs.	Organisation's survey. Appraisals and development interviews. Learning resource centre facilities.

3.5	Effective action takes place to achieve the training and development objectives of individuals and the organisations.	Reviews of objectives achieved – appraisal and interview records. System for appraising and reviewing training – NVQ/SVQ/MCI certificates.
3.6	Managers are actively involved in supporting employees to meet their training and development needs.	Written support from managers within system. Appraisal system – objectives. Manager's job description. Certificate – MCI standards achieved.
4.1	The organisation evaluates how its development of people is contributing to business goals and targets.	Effects of training – team leader evaluates. Overall evaluation – directors/senior managers meetings – minutes. Course evaluation forms.
4.2	The organisation evaluates whether its development actions have achieved their objectives.	Statistics on objectives of business plan. Director/senior manager evaluations from reports surveys, appraisals and courses. Achievement of NVQ/SVQ/MCI.
4.3	The outcomes of training and development are evaluated at individual, team and organisational levels.	Individual – appraisal papers. Team – targets achieved. Organisation – progress evaluated by senior management – minutes. Surveys of employees at organisational level.
4.4	Top management understands the broad costs and benefits of developing people.	Business plan. Adequate training budget. Positive evaluation reports. Increases in productivity.
4.5	The continuing commitment of top	Mission statement and

management to developing people is communicated to all employees.	business plan extracts. Attitudes from surveys. Newsletters.

As she wrote down what she thought would be relevant evidence, Mary had become more confident of her judgement. Like all of the work she had done on IIP, including evaluation, it all seemed to fit into a logical pattern.

She also realised that some of her suggestions might be thought to be over-ambitious for a small company. What value was a survey of a small number of employees? In fact, she had done exactly this and recently had had many suggestions from staff that they might not have made at a meeting. Meetings of directors/senior managers involved only Alex herself, Mary and Phillip, but they still made sense.

The 'message' seemed to be, from Mary's experience, 'have a system' and 'keep documentation on everything'.

Mary's next step was to add additional headings to the matrix she had drawn up so as to bring in more material from her consideration of all the indicators.

Question

If Mary still had doubts about what should be put in or left out of the portfolio, what could she do to obtain help in making a decision?

DISCUSSION POINTS

1. In what kind of situation would an assessor want to interview employees in addition to paper/video evidence? Try to make your example(s) as concrete as possible.

2. Why do you think that the amount of portfolio evidence should depend on quality rather than quality?

3. If some of the portfolio evidence is sensitive or confidential, how would you decide on exactly what the assessor could see?

4. If you were the staff member delegated to compile a portfolio, would you do it all yourself or invite other people to help you? What factors would influence you in making your decision?

9
Writing the Storyboard

The **storyboard** is essentially part of your Investors in People portfolio. It is sometimes called part 1 of the portfolio and is a way of explaining the materials, documents, videos and tapes contained in it.

Put yourself in the position of the assessor. He/she may have made a pre-assessment visit to your organisation and told you about the assessment procedures. But then he/she will need to know about **your** organisation.

This is where the storyboard is most useful. It has three main purposes:

- providing a record of your progress towards IIP
- helping the assessor understand your organisation
- explaining the material in the portfolio.

RECORDING PROGRESS

The storyboard can bring a coherent pattern to the documentary and other evidence in the portfolio. It can genuinely tell a story. Why? Because it is extremely unusual for any organisation which has been working towards IIP for anything between a year and two years to remain totally unchanged.

So the storyboard, like any well produced narrative, has a beginning, a middle and an end – which also marks the start of the next three year period when you will be reassessed for IIP.

You start with the main 'character' in your story – your company or organisation, whether it is public or private, small or large, on one or many sites.

You describe what service the organisation provides or what its products are. Some details of the organisation's 'history' can be very helpful. How many departments, divisions or sections does it have? All this can be illustrated by an organisational chart.

You should turn now to the **people** within the organisation:

- What are their differing levels and specialisms?
- How are people organised?
- Is it still a hierarchical system or is it much flatter?
- Who is the chief executive or managing director?
- Who are the senior managers?
- Is there any HRD group, a finance department, an administrative department, a resource centre, a training group?
- How many production workers or basic operatives are employed?
- What are the aims and targets of the organisation?
- What is the vision for the future?
- What are the specific objectives – increased turnover, profitability, productivity, quality?
- Are the objectives quantifiable – does every member of your business know how he/she contributes to achieving the targets?
- How do you recruit, select, train and retain good staff?

BRIEFING THE ASSESSOR

No doubt, from the facts presented in the portfolio, the assessor could work out much of the above information but it is much easier if he/she is 'steered through' the portfolio information. It is even more effective if, therefore, he/she can meet staff members informally and see them in their normal place of work **before** the official assessment visit takes place.

So the assessor's likely procedure on a pre-assessment visit would be:

- to look through three groups of material – the storyboard, the portfolio, and the organisation chart with all the staff duly named

- to describe to senior staff how the assessment visiting time will be taken up (mainly interviewing staff)
- to explain how staff will be chosen for acquiring the primary evidence, through interviews
- to meet staff informally when walking round the main premises.

So the kind of information described above will be of great value to the assessor, who will have a very clear picture of your organisation even at this stage.

PRESENTING THE STORY

The basic rule in presenting the storyboard is essentially the same as your presentation of evidence. Make it **adequate, clear** and **precise**. Again it does not need to be lengthy – just enough to explain the organisation and the portfolio:

- this is how and when we started
- this is how we proceeded
- this is what happened – interim results – progress towards targets
- this is how we evaluated the IIP programme
- this is the kind of progress we are looking towards.

As you tell the story, refer during the course of your description to each of the papers, videos, memos, audio tapes and other evidence in the portfolio. Refer each of these to the appropriate reference number, *eg* E4 in brackets, in the text immediately after the part of your 'story' which is supported by the evidence. There could of course be several references attaching to some of the themes in your story.

STRUCTURING THE INFORMATION

To illustrate how you might structure the storyboard, we can take as Example A the 'matrix' information in Figure 10 and as Example B the list of indicators with suggested evidence on pages 117 to 121.

The most interesting way of structuring the storyboard would be to write an introduction about the organisation then say exactly how you proceeded as the programme began to take shape. Reference should be made all the time to portfolio material.

EXAMPLE A

PACTEC

Introduction and background

The company was founded by two brothers, James and Donald Withington, who had both worked as skilled electronic supervisors in a long established company which produced televisions and radios. Record players were also a significant element of production which 'took off' in the 1960s.

Both recognised almost simultaneously that one of the causes of slow delivery – apart from inefficiencies in the transport section and the slowing effect of strikes – was the poor quality of packing and resulting breakages.

The process was very slow and time-consuming even though a large staff was employed on this job. An added complication was the slow delivery of component parts from supplier organisations. This often threw the production lines into chaos, especially when a significant part had run out.

So James and Donald decided to set up their own business, providing a specialist packaging service for many different industries, ranging from electronic equipment to food. They were able to use many of the recently developed materials, polythene and polystyrene.

None of this happened by accident. They had done their own market research and discovered a significant niche.

Starting with small premises and five employees, they have gradually built up the business to have several hundred significant customers. In 1996 we have 537 employees, operating from eight sites, and our production methods are second to none. On the other hand, updating has been required in the management of the company. Now there are fewer managers – a chief executive with five seniors and eight site managers. There are also 40 team leaders (A).

Having quite recently been successful with ISO9000 we approached the TEC covering the area of our main site to find out about the details of Investors in People. After several meetings including our top management team and HRD director with staff from the TEC, we set up a representative group of staff including some from other sites, to start planning in detail. The group produced a detailed **action plan** in the form of a statement of what had to be done, by whom and by when (B1).

The senior management group started work on an expanded **business plan** (C2) including detailed aims and objectives. The addition to this of all the accompanying training needs and how these would be met and paid for required a larger and more specific training budget (E1) – not just an overall sum but split up into specific costings, *eg* many of our staff would for the first time be working towards VQs or units of VQs.

COMMITMENT

The directors and senior managers, along with other representatives including the union, then drew up an amended version of our **mission statement** (C1), putting more emphasis on the needs of our customers.

Having made a great deal of progress in just two months, we then formally committed to IIP. Our executive director, James Goodlad, wrote a **letter of commitment** (B2) to the chief executive of the TEC and received an acknowledgement (B3) and Certificate of Commitment (B4).

The TEC do not have a specific form of this letter but, in general, it affirmed our beliefs in the four principles of IIP and our determination to meet the 24 indicators.

Communicating with staff

The next stage was of general inter-communication. All staff on all sites were informed of the commitment to IIP through staff meetings and the organisational newsletter. The mission statement and extracts from the business plan (C2) were given to every member of staff and also the IIP indicators. At large meetings and team meetings these details and our business plan were explained and discussed by James Goodlad, the directors, senior managers and other managers. Similar meetings took place with union representatives.

Employees were also told about a proposal to supplement information about training needs from appraisals (H1, H2) by conducting a survey of the training needs of all employees (F). Details also of our HRD/training policy document (D1, D2) were also circulated and discussed.

Everybody at this stage knew about the details of IIP but a good deal of it still had to be put into practice. The main point was that all the staff were equally involved. There would be constant updatings on what was happening especially if new procedures were to be started.

NB. The above commentary and the portfolio evidence quoted could cover most of the assessment indicators for the commitment section of the IIP requirements.

REVIEW

Although there had been an appraisal system for some of the staff before IIP commenced, the three main features of changes in review of training and development processes were:

- a universal appraisal system – once or twice a year (to be discussed)
- a survey of training needs – and training needs analysis
- a list of relevant VQs and MCI qualifications for staff.

A sub committee of the IIP group was set up to rewrite the appraisal documents (H1) and a new personal development plan document (G2) which reflected ongoing mentoring, development type interviews and meetings with team leaders.

Appraisal forms had to include individual objectives, and specify a VQ qualification to be worked towards.

Everyone has to be totally familiar with these forms, including the kind of issues to be discussed. Both appraiser and appraisee had to be prepared to make suggestions and discuss possibilities.

HRD staff had also been asked to run a course for managers and team leaders on:

- how they should conduct appraisal sessions (including listening skills)
- writing out and summarising aims
- developing an awareness of VQs
- encouraging employees to express themselves (H2).

NB. The above commentary to the portfolio evidence referred to covers part of section 2 of the IIP Standard, Review.

An alternative storyboard format

The second approach to writing the storyboard would be to present the introduction as in the previous version and then take each of the principles and indicators in turn, referring the assessor to the specific indicators covered. We shall outline how we might do this for the first principle – commitment.

EXAMPLE B

Commitment

1.1 There is a public commitment from the most senior level within the organisation to develop people.

Evidence

Letter from James Goodlad, chief executive,
to Robert Naysmith, chief executive of Northshire TEC B2
Acknowledgement of letter from Robert Naysmith B3
Certificate of Commitment B4
James Goodlad's message to the workforce (Newsletter 9/2/96),
including names of IIP working group and summary of the
company's IIP action plan B1

The evidence noted above shows that PACTEC formally committed to

Investors in People by written communication with the TEC. Prior to this, discussions had taken place with the TEC about the ways in which PACTEC should proceed. Work on an action plan was completed before formal commitment was made. The workforce were informed of all these activities through publicity in the newsletter and circulating all staff of the chief executive's letter of commitment and summary of the action plan. Senior managers and team leaders also discussed IIP with various groups on all the sites, representing all the workforce.

1.2 Employees at all levels are aware of the broad aims and vision of the organisation.

Evidence
Organisational mission statement C1
Extracts from the business plan (with statements of aims
over the next three years)..C2
HRD/training policy document D2
Survey of training needs..F

Before formally committing PACTEC to IIP, we distributed to the workforce and publicised widely a new mission statement which expresses more accurately what we now think of as our organisational vision. It places more emphasis on our constant wish to provide what our customers need – the best quality product, delivered as and when the customer requires.
The business plan summary consists of four sections:

- the mission statement – explained in more detail
- the specific aims of the organisation (with clear targets and standards)
- training and development needs in line with the business plan
- where possible, equivalent NVQs or SVQs are listed.

The four further indicators in section 1 are mainly covered by the same evidence:

1.3 There is a written and flexible plan which sets out business goals and targets.
1.4 The plan identifies broad development needs and specifies how they will be assessed and met.
1.5 The employer has considered what employees at all levels would contribute to the success of the organisation and has communicated this effectively to them.
1.6 Where representative structures exist, management communicates with

employee representatives a vision of where the organisation is going and the contributions employees (and their representatives) will make to its success.

The mission statement and business plan were discussed at large and team group meetings as well as what Investors in People means for the company. The work-force were also told of the survey of training needs and of the forms they would be asked to complete. This would confirm and lead to amplification of the training section of the business plan. If additions or changes were made to the business plan, employees would be informed as quickly as possible. Special meetings between management and the trade union representatives showed complete agreement on the desirability of the company achieving Investors in People. Also circulated was a new HRD/training policy document showing how all staff are entitled to training.

Whichever of the two approaches to the storyboard that you take, you should of course then go on to cover all the other indicators.

Writing up action evidence

This could include the actions you have taken in your drive to achieve the IIP Standard. But mainly it is about action taken towards an excellent training and development system, *eg* the setting up of or improvements to your induction system. You could provide evidence for the assessment of training after induction by including in the portfolio examples of individual training plans and personal development plans. The latter could also include a running record of training required for coping with new company projects or products. Descriptions of such special courses for staff could include the content of the course and the methodology.

Writing up evaluation evidence

Here you could include a description of how your organisation evaluates training at different levels – top management, team/departmental and individual level. Make sure that what you write matches the evidence in the portfolio. If a survey of training needs has been carried out and an evaluation section within it has produced useful information, your storyboard should describe these results, especially the general evaluation which can be made.

KEEPING THE RIGHT BALANCE

As well as the two approaches so far described which can be taken in writing the storyboard, another way would be to use specific process headings, such as 'Appraisals', 'The business plan', or 'Staff involvement'. Remember that the reason for the storyboard is to provide the assessor with a clear picture of your organisation, its reasons for viewing IIP as a worthwhile strategy, how you embarked on a programme and evaluated the results of training and development as part of IIP in the success of the business.

One of the most difficult parts of writing the storyboard is just how much detail to go into. Again, the best policy is to write enough to steer the reader through your organisation – its development, structure, aims and vision – and through the story of your progress towards Investors in People. If you can in this process provide figures on:

- increased productivity
- increased turnover
- better quality
- lower staff turnover
- increased staff morale
- big increase in staff qualifications
- other measures of success

then this is a powerful argument for your case that it is IIP which has produced these marked positive effects. Better still, if you have 'before IIP' and 'after IIP' facts and statistics relating to improved business, then this would make your portfolio stand out as illustrating real organisational success.

Remember to keep the right balance between:

- too much/too little detail
- over-optimistic/very down-played comments
- too much/too little evidence (three pieces of evidence for each indicator is adequate – oral or written).

Presenting the storyboard effectively

Presentation of the storyboard can make a big difference to your apparent effectiveness. Use of desk-top publishing and clear illustrations and diagrams can make for especially clear presentation and readability. Interviews with your workforce will either support or contradict your write-up. You should try to ensure that written and interview evidence should largely match each other – through the kind of communication we have discussed earlier.

SUMMARY

- The main reasons for writing a storyboard.
- Shaping the storyboard – beginning, middle and end.
- Briefing the assessor – the organisation structure and its staff.
- Presenting the story: examples.
- Writing up systems as they developed.
- Providing relevant business statistics to show effects of Investors in People.

CASE STUDY

Vernon shows his diplomacy

Nearly 15 months had elapsed since Vernon, Ryan and Sue, the HRD group at PACTEC, had started the company on its IIP programme. They had been very successful so far, they thought, in two ways – improving the appraisal, induction and other processes, especially evaluating training and shifting the company culture to put much more emphasis on the line manager as an appraiser and trainer, leaving HRD to have a more strategic planning function. Now they had arrived at a point where they believed they could ask the TEC for help with a trial assessment.

'Of course', Ryan observed, 'we don't really have to have a trial assessment now if they feel confident we're on the right lines, but it would be very helpful to us to get outside confirmation.'

'It's possible they'll nominate a consultant to do it.'

'Just to tidy up', said Vernon, 'have we got most people briefed on their contributions during the assessment – the kind of questions they could be asked? Oh, and Sue, how's the portfolio – have you managed to find all the documentation? Have you documented all the details of the training related to the business plan?'

'The answer is yes and no', replied Sue. 'I think I have nearly all the documentation now, but I don't think it's necessary to put all the details of training in with the business plan.'

'Well it depends', observed Vernon, 'on what you mean by detail. I don't think you should detail every small bit of a training course on say our new machinery, or copy out everything on the engineering VQ, but you should at least list all the VQs and supply general outlines of specific courses.'

'Well, I don't agree', said Sue. 'I was proposing to write down only the fact we were being assessed against the criteria of the main VQs.'

'Okay, I'll check on this', said Vernon, although he was sure already that he was right.

However, Vernon didn't want to annoy Sue because she had done a great deal of very thorough work.

Question

Who do you think was right in this controversy?

DISCUSSION POINTS

1. Much of the documented evidence could be provided through answers to the assessor's questions. Particularly with small companies, such oral evidence could be regarded as valid, even with the principle of commitment. Do you think that you would be confident enough that everyone on your staff would be able to confirm what their colleagues had said? How could you ensure as far as possible that they would agree?

2. Do you think that any single member of staff of an organisation of 100+ people could by themselves gather all the relevant papers for IIP? If not, what other method could be used to gather information consistently?

3. How would you decide on the way in which the storyboard should be written and presented? Would the IIP group leader make the decision or should it be on the majority opinion of the IIP group?

4. Do you think that the requirements for IIP assessment are too bureaucratic or do you take the view that compiling a portfolio and writing the storyboard is a rewarding process?

10
Conducting Staff Appraisals

CHANGING THE CONCEPT OF APPRAISALS

Dealing with gaps in competency

The traditional view of the appraisal as being a one-way criticism by the manager of personnel department of the employee's weaknesses – with perhaps a little on strengths – is no longer tenable. If weaknesses are now seen as improvable by training, negative attitudes towards appraisal lessen or disappear. Again, if training is required, it is highly desirable that agreement is reached on *exactly* what is needed and how it will be carried out.

Coping with disagreement

If agreement on necessary training is not possible, then the disagreements should be documented at the end of the appraisal form, with both the manager and the appraisee writing down their points of view. A senior manager can then arbitrate and decide what can be done to settle the problem.

It is clearly important that **appraisal forms** should be included in the portfolio. It may be more difficult because of confidentiality to include completed appraisal forms. It would be absolutely necessary for an employee's permission to be given before a written-up appraisal form could be included.

DOCUMENTING APPRAISALS

We have already covered the purpose of appraisals but the whole process must be carried out within a consistent context, *ie* the use of a **standard** form or booklet. These can vary in format according to type and level of the job, although there may be some core elements necessary for every member of staff.

A booklet can be divided up as follows:

- essential details – name, job title
- rating scales on job skills, competences and behavioural qualities
- comments on the ratings or the skills/competences/behaviours
- comments on previous personal objectives reached or not reached
- self ratings
- objectives for the future.

Rating scales

Your appraisal form could contain a series of scales where the particular skills, competences and personal attributes needed for the job are assessed by the appraiser.

As an example, suppose that 'the ability to work under pressure' is a very important part of the job and the line manager knows the appraisee well enough to assess the employee on this.

He/she will have to decide where the employee is placed on this type of scale.

Works calmly, quietly and effectively in stressful circumstances				Becomes emotional and works much less effectively when under pressure
A	B	C	D	E

The end points are defined and you as the appraiser must choose A, B, C, D, E or intermediate points. Would you be accurate?

You must ask yourself:

- What is C – an average level of emotion?
- How would my ratings compare with those of other appraisers?

Training appraisers

This is why training and experience in appraising are of such importance. To be able to assess as well as possible you would need instructional sessions where the meaning of 'the ability to work under pressure' would be properly discussed. Sample case studies would be considered and a rating agreed upon. Videos of simulated interviews could be discussed. Such courses can help to increase the reliability (consistency) and validity (accuracy of assessment).

As an alternative to rating scales, the manager/appraiser can write down what *they* themselves think. Under a heading like 'employee's strengths' they could write:

- Shows persistence and determination.
- Excellent awareness of customer needs.
- Very good at listening.
- Has high level of computer skills.
- Shows good leadership potential.

These phrases tend to be subjective but can, in the hands of an experienced appraiser, be very useful. Notice that they describe behaviour which can be changed rather than fixed adjectives, *eg* lazy, clever.

Using the opposite heading of 'employee's weaknesses', possible comments could be:

- Tells customers what they want without listening first.
- Does not co-operate well with team.
- Uses colleagues' ideas without giving them credit.
- Has arrogant manner with subordinates.
- Lacks expertise in . . .

Remember, however, that it is best to discuss comments like these with the appraisee first of all before writing down anything formally.

APPRAISING: WHO, WHERE AND HOW?

Who?

The appraiser and appraisee are involved in a one-to-one confidential interview of which a record is kept. The appraiser is probably a line manager but may be in personnel or HRD. He/she must be trained so as to ensure that all appraisers are doing the same job in the same way, including the proper interpretation of rating scales.

Where?

It is important that appraisals are carried out in a quiet, private room where the conversation cannot be overheard or body language be assessed from a distance. It is probably best to be in as **familiar setting** as possible for both parties and that a desk does not come between the two. Note taking should be done as unobtrusively as possible and written into official forms at a later point.

How?

The atmosphere should be as **relaxed** and non-stressful as possible. If both appraiser and appraisee have done their homework, the process should be satisfactory and even enjoyable. It is very important that throughout the appraisal both people involved keep a note of what has been agreed as they go along and that at the end of the interview summing up is carried out in some detail and once again agreed. Both people should sign the document and then complete it with any comments, positive or negative. In particular, any disagreements should be written up and signed.

ACTIONING THE DECISIONS

The most important of the areas to be covered during appraisal is that of future **agreed objectives**. These could be as relatively straightforward as the appraisee acquiring a vocational qualification.

But human relations objectives could also be included, for example:

- to improve customer relations by learning to listen carefully
- to develop team skills and to learn a specific team role
- to learn the skills of instructing and coaching and to display these in practical situations
- to develop positive relationships with colleagues at all levels.

It is precisely these kinds of objectives that are difficult to discuss except within an appraisal system. To achieve this degree of reality, both appraiser and appraisee must be aware of the practicalities of the system. **Before** the interview, employees should be asked to think about their strengths and weaknesses and any training needed.

Collecting portfolio evidence

Training for managers in all of the processes of appraisal, induction, mentoring and instructing should be supported by evidence for the portfolio, *eg* programmes of courses, course handouts, certificates and course evaluation forms. Since the most important part of the assessment process for IIP is a programme of interviews by the assessor with staff, managers should be able to answer questions and discuss points on all aspects of working with people.

SUMMARY

- Appraisals along with selection induction and career counselling are a very important part of an organisation's progress towards Investors in People. If you already have an appraisal system, try to link it more closely to training and development.

- Appraisals must be linked to organisational objectives. Progress with objectives linked to the previous appraisal should be discussed and the process evaluated. Strengths and weaknesses of the appraisee should be discussed frankly.

- Both the organisation and the individual benefit from this kind of constructive discussion – relevant training helps organisational flexibility and useful qualifications can be obtained by the appraisee.

- At the end of the interview the appraisers should sum this up, stating again the agreed objectives. Conclusions should be summarised at the end of the document.

- Every effort should be made to keep sensitive issues as confidential as possible. If a completed appraisal form is to be used to provide IIP evidence it should be with the permission of the appraisees concerned.

CASE STUDY

Vernon wins the next round

'This "Investors in People" type appraisal suits me very well', observed Vernon. 'I've never liked making employees of PACTEC unnecessarily miserable over fear of what kind of criticism you are going to throw at them.'

'That wouldn't worry me too much', said his assistant, Ryan. 'Giving people a bit of a fright can motivate them and do them quite a lot of good.'

'Anyway', said Vernon, 'we now have to hand over a lot of our appraisal interviewing programme to the line managers. I know you have already written out a one day course. Do you have a draft timetable for it?'

'Yes, I do', agreed Ryan. 'I could start with a one hour lecture on appraisals. Then we could give them some case studies to work out for themselves. After lunch they could see the video and after that I suggest a multiple choice test.'

Vernon was a little taken aback at this rather tough and, in his opinion, ineffectual programme.

'Sounds just okay', he said, 'but I have one or two other suggestions which I think will improve it.'

'Oh', said Ryan huffily, 'I think my ideas are excellent.'

'Here would be my programme', said Vernon, showing Ryan the details he had sketched-out:

1. Video a good example of two-way appraisal interviewing.
2. Discussion of how the interview was handled and the good points.
3. Discussion on our new format for appraisal and meanings of rating scales so that everyone agrees on them.
4. Groups of three people agree on how they would use the new format to appraise an imaginary employee, with a very detailed description of his/her work. Discussion on how different groups rated the employee. Try to agree in conclusions.
5. Managers in pairs appraise each other with total realism, *ie* experience in peer assessment.
6. Discussion on arrangements – how appraisals are to be scheduled – who signs the forms – where appraisals are stored – who has access – who summarises recommendations so that senior management see the trends in training needs – the completion of personal development plans – who keeps them?

After Ryan had finished reading this programme he asked, 'What, no exam!'

'No', said Vernon, for once decisively. 'We're not testing knowledge, we're assessing the appraiser's interviewing skills – although they do need to know quite a lot about VQs and other courses. I think that an exam would be totally unnecessary.'

'I don't agree', protested Ryan, as he slammed the door on the way out.

Question

Discuss with colleagues why you think either Vernon or Ryan was correct in their views of the right kind of course. Is Vernon's course adequate? Has he covered all that needs to be covered?

DISCUSSION POINTS

1. Some organisations have two appraisals – one for reviewing training and development needs and one for performance related pay. Are you in favour of this system?

2. Do you think that individual appraisals have extra advantages beyond training needs identification, *eg* employees like to be considered as individuals?

3. Do you think that reviewing training needs in terms of the business plan and how far employees are competent to achieve its objectives is a better strategy than training being regarded as 'a good thing' but without real purpose?

4. Do you agree that the appraisal (or development) interview is a much better process than the traditional 'critical appraisal'?

11
Being Assessed

PREPARING FOR ASSESSMENT

The important point to remember is that the assessor's aim is to find out if all the processes relating to the assessment indicators are in place and really happening.

After a year or 18 months of work towards reaching the Standard, you may begin to think that your organisation is ready for assessment. Nearly all the indicators seem to you to have been covered by activities ranging from inducting staff to evaluating training and development programmes. This by itself, however, is not enough.

Arranging training sessions

At the same time as your IIP group have been organising the formal requirements of the Standard, they should also have been preparing staff for the assessment process. This preparation takes quite a long time. You cannot afford to wait till a week or two before your real assessment happens or even a pre-assessment check on your present 'state of health'. So even before a 'trial assessment' or pre-assessment practice run, usually carried out by a member of staff from the TEC/LEC, you yourselves should have an organisational rehearsal or a series of sessions with all the various groups of staff – different sites and departments.

Updating employees

During the whole of your Investors programme, you will have been keeping everyone in your organisation informed of progress – at group meetings where IIP is a permanent item on every agenda. Nearer the actual assessment, however, you should have a series of meetings dealing with the assessment process itself.

The IIP working group for your organisation should convey to everyone the basics of the assessment:

- the portfolio and storyboard – the headings and the type of evidence

- the system by which the assessor asks questions during individual interviews and group meetings.

Taking the first of these points, the employees could be reminded that there is now an appraisal process for all employees where they can discuss with their line manager their training needs and agree on objectives to be achieved before the next appraisal. It may be that mostly these objectives are a continuation of previous ones rather than being completely different. Few employees require radical new objectives every year or six months.

Employees can also be reminded of the induction system, and any other processes by which training needs are actively catered for and supported by their managers, and of other processes covered in the organisation's IIP portfolio.

Organising employee discussions

During such meetings it is an excellent idea to organise discussions involving smaller groups of six to eight members of staff, covering their views on these new processes, how they themselves have been affected and whether they think they have had positive effect on production and morale.

Topics at group level could be about the organisation:

- Is the organisation really committed to IIP?
- Do we know of the vision and mission of the organisation?
- Does the appraisal system work well?
- Are managers/team leaders competent in appraising, inducting and instructing their staff?
- Are we properly trained for our existing job or for new jobs?
- Are we made aware of training opportunities?
- Does evaluation of training lead to improvements?

Feedback on the results of these discussions to management can help to decide whether the whole organisation is ready for IIP assessment.

Preparing to answer relevant questions

Employees could be told that part of the assessment process involves the assessor interviewing some of them individually or in a group, and they could be asked questions such as:

- Do you know your role in furthering the organisation's vision and aims?
- Are your individual training needs discussed?
- Have you had appropriate training?
- Were you involved in evaluating training?
- Has your manager discussed your training with you?
- Has he/she helped you put it into practice?

Questions such as these can be discussed and suggestions made on how they could be answered. Of course it would be a mistake to attempt to have employees 'swot up the answers'. They would come across as having been given the form of words and it would lack genuineness and spontaneity. On the other hand, an awareness of how, generally, to get one's ideas together and speak to a particular topic is very well worth while.

PUTTING ASSESSMENT IN CONTEXT

When you think you are ready for assessment, your chief executive or managing director will apply to the TEC or LEC. The latter usually need background information on factors like location, type of site, types of job, staff representatives, the number of full-time or part-time jobs. Other types of information would be total number of employees, male or female, how long in employment with this organisation, employees with special needs, ethnic origin, and length of service statistics.

Costs

All organisations want to know how to cost the whole process. Generally assessments cost £550 a day + VAT and the assessor's expenses. 'Time' is not just the amount required by the assessor to inspect the portfolio and to talk to groups and individuals, but also the time it takes him/her to compile the report, and the initial familiarisation process so he or she has an accurate picture of the organisation itself.

Some enterprise companies vary rates to small businesses and charities and could provide an estimate of costs.

The assessor

The person who assesses you is employed by a recognition unit, part of a national network, run in England and Wales by the TECs, by the Training and Enterprise Agency in Northern Ireland, by Investors in People, Scotland, in Scotland and by Investors in People UK. He/she will be based in the unit nearest to your main building. If your organisation is on one site only then probably you will have one assessor from the recognition unit of the local TEC or from IIP Scotland Ltd. If your organisation covers fewer than five sites, it is assessed by the local TEC unit co-ordinated by the lead TEC unit (where the HQ site is situated). If your organisation covers five or more TEC areas, then you can be assessed by your own TEC unit with a project team of local TEC units (from the five) and/or national assessors (IIP UK), or by each local TEC unit if each site has a separate business plan and a good deal of autonomy. In Scotland the assessors on multiple sites would be employed by IIP Scotland.

Knowing the procedure

What are the main processes in assessments? These will probably be explained to you by the assessor on a pre-assessment visit. Whereas a trial or pre-assessment may take the form of interviews with a group of employees with, possibly, a scan over the portfolio, on the actual assessment there is a well scheduled process:

- The assessor will look at, either on the premises or at base, the portfolio and storyboard. He/she may construct their own 'matrix' to ensure that every process will have taken place by checking indicators against evidence.

- In agreement with the organisation being assessed, he/she will arrange an interview schedule with employees. The number of staff interviewed depends on the various degrees of autonomy of different working groups as well as on total numbers, but what follows is based on the total number:

Number of staff employed	*Sample band (%)*
0–5	100%
6–15	60–80%
16–25	40–70%
26–50	30–60%
51–75	25–50%
76–100	20–40%
100–125	15–30%
126–500	10–20%
501–1000	5–15%
1001–2500	4–8%
2501–5000	2–4%
5000+	1–3%

In deciding how large a sample to interview, the assessor would take into account, in addition to total numbers of staff and type of site, the number of types of job levels in the organisation, the details of the portfolio evidence and responses to survey data.

After studying the portfolio and storyboard thoroughly, the assessor decides how many staff at which levels to interview. He/she will inform your organisation of the proposed assessment schedule including names of staff, and you, as an organisation, will be able to draw up a programme, including accommodation to be used.

The reasons for an interview programme are:

- to clarify any points in the portfolio which are ambiguous or do not refer clearly to an indicator
- to obtain extra particulars if the portfolio evidence appears to be insufficient
- to enable the assessor to decide if the standard has been met on a specific indicator
- to talk about and discuss with employees and their managers to check that the processes actually work and that employees really

believe that the organisation is committed to their training and development.

The term 'interview' can be misleading. An assessor does not have to interview all staff individually in a separate room.

Interviewing approaches

As the purpose of interviews is to expand on and check portfolio evidence, the assessor is as informal as possible with all the participants. Indeed this part of the procedure is gaining in importance because of its practical validity. Interviews can take place in the areas where the staff normally work so as to ensure they are more at ease. Similarly, 'interviews' can often be more like conversations where questions are just part of the general discussion. The reaction of most staff, who can sometimes be unnecessarily worried, is that the whole process has been quite pleasant – nothing like the ordeal they had feared.

Such fears can be alleviated by the IIP Working Group, who can confirm the general informality of the procedures.

The assessor must have for interview a significant sample of the whole staff including:

- the **managing director/chief executive** (always), to find out if the latter can clearly expand on the connection between business objectives and targets with training and development

- **senior managers**, to explain how they put general policy into specific actions

- **personnel/HRD/training managers**, to discuss the way they can help train all types of managers to adapt to the strategy

- **line managers**, to discuss with the assessors how they coach and develop people in their groups

- **union representatives**, where appropriate, to discuss their contribution to training and development policy

- **individual employees**, to confirm that the business really is committed to developing them so as to achieve its vision.

The assessor can also speak to other groups:

- very **recent employees** who can be asked about their induction
- a **chain of employees**, *ie* from group senior manager to line manager or team leader to employees, who are all involved in the same process.

Do not forget that some employees, canteen workers and cleaners can sometimes be forgotten, but they too must be included in the IIP process if they are employees of the organisation.

Checking training records and personal development plans

The assessor may have seen an example in the portfolio of an individual training record. In it there could be a progression of training processes for the individual. He/she can then interview that person to ask about how their training needs were identified, what processes were followed, what training and development actions taken, the courses evaluated and the ways in which the team leader put the employee's new learning into use. Alternatively, the assessor could study the training or personal development plans of the staff he proposes to interview, and then check with them if these plans have been followed through. This is where the earlier suggestion that employees should have updated copies of their own plans would be very useful.

Presenting documentation

Either at the pre-assessment visit or on the first day of the assessment, the assessor should be allocated a room where he/she can study the portfolio and storyboard.

The portfolio can be a single expanding file or a series of individually categorised files, and the storyboard, cross-referenced to the file, should be a well produced booklet printed in as effective a format as possible, desk-top published with clear tables and illustrations. This, along with an organisational chart, is all that the assessor needs to form a preliminary opinion of the adequacy of the evidence and to be able to draw up a list of a representative group of staff to be interviewed.

Helping with the interview schedule

Once the assessor has notified you of the staff he/she wishes to interview, you can then check if they are available. Some may be off ill and others could be away on business visits. These are not serious problems since the assessor will probably have put more staff on the list than is actually required – just in case some people may not be able to attend.

Depending on whether the assessor wishes to see the staff

individually or in a group, you can arrange a schedule of interviews including the rooms required. Directors and heads of departments will be interviewed alone and in their own rooms.

ANSWERING THE ASSESSOR'S QUESTIONS

In this section we will consider the types of questions and discussion points that the assessor could introduce. It is not suggested that you memorise specific answers, but it would be sensible for all levels of staff to prepare in general terms what they could say in reply. The more aware staff are of the company's vision and plans and the details of IIP, the more certain that they will be able to do well. As ever, preparation and excellent communication ensure the best pay-off.

Each of the kinds of questions an assessor may ask would be considered under the four principles of IIP.

1. Commitment

Most of the questions on this principle will be directed towards the managing director/chief executive and top level managers.

- Do your employees know about and understand your commitment to Investors in People?

- How do you plan business strategy? Is the plan updated? How do you translate aims into the skills, abilities and qualifications that your employees will require?

- Do your staff know in general terms the meaning of your mission statement, and some of the main details of your business plan?

- How are employees informed of their individual contribution to the business?

- How do you ensure that management have an effective communication system with employees?

For employees

- Do you think that management have a real commitment to training and developing all employees so that the business plan's objectives are reached?

- What is your organisation trying to achieve?
- What are some of the goals of the organisation?
- How do *you* contribute to reaching the goals?
- How does *your* work relate to your organisation's objectives?
- Are you able to suggest how the company could improve its performance towards its aims and objectives?

2. Review

For managing directors

- Who is responsible in your organisation for training and development?
- Are you convinced that training needs at all levels should be related to the company's aims and goals?
- How often during a year should training needs be reviewed against goals?
- How are your managers' people skills assessed against your objectives?
- Do you have a policy on the training of people with special needs?

For senior managers

- Do you know your share of the training budget?
- Do you review training needs regularly? Are individual employees able to put forward their ideas on training?
- Do you relate training needs to external qualifications? If so can you provide some examples?
- Who is responsible for training and development needs of senior managers?

- Have you had any training yourself in people management?
- How much does training and development cost each year?

For managers

- Do you think that training and development are important topics during team meetings?
- Do you think that taking appraisals has led to improved motivation?
- If business needs change, is it an automatic process for you to review training?
- Are all employees' needs reviewed?

For employees

- What is *your* role in the business?
- Are your training needs reviewed? How is this done?
- Who is the person responsible for your training and development?
- Are your managers able to assess your training needs and development effectively?
- Are there equal opportunities for training in this organisation?
- Is the training you have had relevant to *your* job?
- Are objectives agreed with you and later checked to see if you have achieved them?

3. Action

For managing directors

- Do you have an induction programme for new senior managers?
- Do they work towards specific targets, *eg* MCI?

For senior managers

- Do you check on whether line managers are really involved in employee training?
- How exactly are new recruits inducted into this organisation?
- Are employees given relevant information on training opportunities?
- Is this pursued effectively? Are they encouraged to take up training and development opportunities?
- Could you tell me about your appraisal system?

For line managers

- How far is training and needs assessment carried out on the job?
- Are you included in NVQ/SVQ assessment?
- Do you monitor training and development?
- Do you discuss training before, during and after it occurs?
- Are you really personally involved, *eg* in mentoring?

For employees

- Were you inducted into the organisation? Was the process evaluated?
- What training have you had recently, within six months to a year?
- Have you been informed of training opportunities relevant to you?
- Is your training discussed with you before, during and after training?
- Are you always trained in line with your training/action/personal development plan?

4. Evaluation

For managing directors

- How do you evaluate effects of training on the business as a whole and specifically in relation to the business plan?
- How are overall business development objectives related to training policies?
- Are employees told about major successes in training?
- Are employees/unions told about business successes?
- As the MD, do you see a clear connection between your strategy and continuing training and development?
- What do you see as the main benefits to your organisation emerging from Investors in People?

For senior managers

- How do you evaluate training and development?
- How are line managers involved in evaluating training?
- Is training evaluated in relation to its effect on meeting business goals?
- Is the effect of training evaluated in terms of before and after?
- Is progress towards training objectives monitored?
- What are the criteria you use in calculating the effects of training?

For line managers

- How do you evaluate individual and group training effects?
- How do you check that training is being applied?
- How do you obtain feedback on training and development courses?

- Do you get feedback from trainees?
- How do you assess individual and group contributions to business goals?
- Do you use external standards in evaluating individual and group training processes?

For employees

- What are the aims of the Investors in People Standard? Do you know the four main principles?
- Were you told about the organisation's commitment to training and development of staff?
- Are *you* convinced that this commitment is a real one?
- Have you heard recently about any training successes or new initiatives in training in your business recently?
- Are there lengthy periods of time when nothing is said about training and development?
- Do periods of business recession have any effect on the training offered?
- Do such periods mean that appraisals are not consistently arranged?

Commenting positively

You will realise that the actual questions may not be exactly the same as those quoted above. Some may be woven into general discussions. You can see, however, their significance for IIP. As long as you and the rest of your staff can converse positively on topics such as these – sometimes put to them in a more down-to-earth way – you can be reasonably sure that they will do well in the assessment process.

SUMMARY

- Pre-assessment checks and training sessions.

- Group discussions on changes and improvements because of IIP.
- Familiarising employees with types of questions asked by the assessor and with assessor-led discussions.
- Costs of assessment.
- Details of the assessment process – how samples of employees are selected for interview – reasons for interviews and discussions.
- Assessor follows a process through, *eg* appraisal objectives to subsequent training. Has the system worked? Interviewing employees via an internal 'employee chain' as part of a process (administrative or production).

CASE STUDY

Ken shows the way

Ken Hill was in the midst of coping with a delegation from the administrative staff. They had always been unenthusiastic about IIP, partly because they had never been fully persuaded that it was worth while. Now a more immediate problem presented itself.

'We don't feel at all confident about answering the assessor's questions', said Nora Thomson.

'And I'm so nervous', said Jacquie Gibson, 'that I don't think I'll be able to speak.'

'I may be so sick', said Janet Scott, 'that I won't be able to come into work.'

Ken tried to help reduce their anxieties.

'There's absolutely no need for any anxieties', he observed. 'I've heard that Nichola Elliot is a very fair assessor. All she wants to make sure of is that we have a system and that it works. We don't need to be brilliant. It doesn't need to be really outstanding practice – just enough to meet the Standard.'

'But we don't know exactly what's in the portfolio or the storyboard well enough – we typed it out, but we can't remember it properly', protested Nora.

'But, but,' spluttered Ken, 'you don't need to memorise everything – in fact that would be the worst thing to do. As long as you can talk intelligently – that's the main thing. In fact, it wouldn't really matter if we didn't have a huge portfolio – as long as we do what is required for IIP.'

'But what do we need to do?' asked Nora.

Ken thought for a minute. 'Let's sit down and have a little talk about IIP', he said quietly. 'Nora, what is the main purpose of this organisation?'

'To encourage people and given them practical advice on setting up their own business – to help them arrange finance – to arrange for them to have training in business – book-keeping, buying economically and monitoring cash flow.'

'Good', said Ken. 'Jacquie, what is your particular contribution to our business aims?'

'To provide administrative backing as a group to all the staff involved.'

'And you, individually?'

'My specialism is good presentation of our organisational documentation using desk-top publishing.'

'Did you have any training for this?'

'Oh yes, we all had a special one week course.'

'Do you have regular reviews of your training?'

'Of course, we all have six monthly appraisals from Nora and she is appraised by you.'

'And do you have any NVQs?'

'Oh yes, when they started up, we all did a Level 2 in Business Administration. It was quite easy because of all our experience, but some parts were new to us.'

'And has this continued?'

'Oh yes! We're now all on Level 4 and after that, who knows, we might get to do HNCs and HNDs.'

'There you are,' said Ken, 'you do know how to speak to the assessor.'

'You haven't asked me anything yet', said Janet.

'Okay', said Ken. 'Would you say that Nora is good in her role as appraiser?'

'Oh definitely', said Janet. 'She reads up all the latest information on VQs and brochures for training managers and from the local FE college, and the Business Management department of the university. We're very lucky to have her as a line manager. And, of course, she took a course in appraising two years ago.'

'Are you more confident now?' asked Ken.

The chorus of agreement was really quite reassuring.

'I think I'll ask the rest of the staff the same sort of questions', thought Ken.

Question

Was Ken right to rehearse staff in this way? Should he have insisted they memorise a 'company answer' or should he not have done anything at all and let them find out when the assessor appeared what kind of discussion they would have?

DISCUSSION POINTS

1. If you had several sites in your business, how could you ensure that they were all kept up-to-date on progress on Investors in People and briefed on the assessment process?

2. Do you think that the assessment process as described here is likely to be 'valid' and 'reliable'?
   Valid means that the process will assess what it is meant to assess, *eg* will portfolio evidence and interviews show convincingly that the organisation really does conform to IIP requirements.
   Reliable means that the assessment is consistent, *eg* would different assessors arrive at the same result?

3. Supposing that when employees were questioned that they gave negative answers to the assessor, *eg* No, our training needs are not reviewed. No, we don't think the organisation is really committed to our training and development. Is there anything, as a manager, you could do about this?

4. Do you think that the assessment process as described here is likely to be both fair and accurate? Can you identify any specific faults in it?

12
Decision Making and Re-recognition

THE ASSESSOR – WRITING THE REPORT

After the assessor has completed the portfolio review and interviewing of staff, he/she then has to write a report which will in its final form be submitted to the Recognition Panel – the group of people who recommend whether an organisation should be recognised or not.

So right away the assessor, working from notes, will start analysing the evidence relating to each of the assessment indicators. Is it sufficient to meet this indicator? Does the oral evidence confirm or contradict the portfolio evidence?

There may also be comments or quotations on the portfolio and storyboard relating to an indicator.

Decision processes

In the report also will be background information about the organisation – size, sites, departments, divisions, numbers of employees and so on. All such information, especially financial, will be treated as totally private and confidential.

Next the assessor will write down his/her opinions of whether the evidence is sufficient to achieve the Standard or not.

One possibility would be that during the assessment processes, one or more gaps, some of them basic, will have been identified. If so the assessor can:

- ask for more supporting evidence immediately
- advise exactly on how to remedy the fault
- cease the process for a short time – one or two months – and then return to continue the assessment.

Circumstances like these will be detailed in the report. If, however, the assessor has a clear-cut view on the visit, the normal process is for the completed report to be passed on to an internal verifier – the same role as that found in the VQ system – who acts as a general scrutineer of the consistency and quality of the report.

If there are fundamental problems, *eg* of commitment or culture, then the assessor can recommend a full reassessment with an updated portfolio. He/she would have to discuss this with the organisation.

PRESENTING THE FINDINGS

At the meeting of the Recognition Panel, the assessor acts as an advocate for the organisations which he/she has recommended as having reached the Standard.

The panel consists of four people, representing the Board of the lead TEC or, in Scotland and Northern Ireland, the areas of business, education and the public sector, and is chaired by an experienced member of the panel.

ANSWERING PANEL QUESTIONS

Panel members will have received their copies of the report some five days before the meeting. They will have read it closely and carefully.

Having listened to the assessor put forward his or her case, they can question him/her on any points they wish to follow up from their scrutiny of the report. It could simply be on factors like number of employees in a particular group, or on the adequacy of evidence on the indicators or a gap which they see as possibly significant. It could be a question on scoping, *ie* information covering a number of different divisions, sites or branches in a widespread business or possibly within a franchise operation. (Franchises can be treated as one large organisation or as a number of small businesses.)

Training the panel member

Panel members themselves will be well trained, having attached a workshop and having shadowed a member of a panel during real meetings, followed by mentoring-type discussions.

Whilst carrying out their role, members of the panel keep in mind that:

- all stages of assessment have been properly carried through
- satisfactory evidence has been provided by the assessor to cover all the elements of the Standards

Qualifications of Assessors

An assessor can be an employee of a TEC, IIP UK, IIP Scotland, Training and Employment Agency in Northern Ireland or a contracted consultant. To become qualified (starting after March 1995), the trainee assessor must:

- agree on an initial development plan with TEC/Assessment unit manager
- attend an assessor workshop provided by a licensed training provider
- update the PDP to include mentoring or work shadowing
- register with an IPD Approved Centre
- satisfy a senior assessor that the PDP has been implemented.

At this stage the trainee assessor:

- will undertake the first assessment
- will be assessed as competent on the job against TDLB Unit E11.

If successful he/she becomes an approved assessor and will be notified by the IPD.

Finally, an approved assessor needs to present a portfolio of evidence to their senior assessor and be assessed positively against units E11 and E31 within one year of being an approved assessor.

In mid 1995 there were fewer than 400 assessors in the UK.

Fig. 11. The qualifications of assessors.

- that recognitions are consistent over time, *ie* assessment is reliable
- that the organisation is sufficiently independent as a business to be assessed properly.

The panel during the meeting will have listened closely to the assessor, asked relevant questions, analysed the answers and come to a conclusion.

The decision of the panel is communicated as quickly as possible to the appropriate TEC/LEC/E&TA (Northern Ireland) and IIP. The lead TEC/LEC will inform the head of the organisation.

PROVIDING AN OPINION

If the assessor has decided that the organisation has met all the indicators sufficiently to be recognised he/she will say so and give reasons for that opinion. For example, each indicator can be assessed as having been reached or as having been 'more than reached'. If all the criteria are in the latter category, as far as the assessor is concerned, it would be difficult for the panel to disagree with an overall positive assessment. However, where quite a number of the indicators have only just been reached, the panel may require more information so as to be fully convinced.

Providing an opinion, however, is as far as the assessor can go for he/she will have presented their report in as clear and non jargon-type language as possible. It is the panel's decision which is the final one.

THE ORGANISATION – PREPARING FOR REASSESSMENT/ RE-RECOGNITION

Immediately after the assessment procedure and the results of the Recognition Panel are conveyed to the organisation, feedback will be provided by the assessor. If the organisation has had a negative decision, the feedback will be even more necessary so that the organisation can put things right as soon as possible before re-applying.

Using the assessor's report and feedback

Even of the assessor has recommended to the panel that the organisation is recognisable for Investors in People, at least one or two of the indicators will probably have been identified by the panel as less soundly covered by the evidence than others. Conversely, positive feedback on good or adequate systems will also be given.

During the feedback session to the successful organisation, the assessor can comment on the more and less positive coverage of certain indicators. So, whenever the assessment process has been completed the process towards re-recognition can begin. This is a slight exaggeration because the formal presentation will have to take place, probably a few weeks after the official panel recognition. Staff should be allowed to celebrate for that time at least.

Continuing change

If, however, all the processes have become 'normal', this continuing process should make little difference. Inductions and appraisals, if occurring normally, would still continue. Investors in People is not a static process. It is one of continuing adaptation and change. Once achieved it should continue to help your business to improve.

The aim of the re-recognition is to enable the organisation to prove that it continues to meet the Standard and has done so throughout the period.

Reassessment will take place in three year's time, *ie* within the period of three years. Exceptionally, this period could be extended by up to three months. Reassessment, like assessment, should reflect continued improvement. Through using the same and probably additional criteria you will be able to compare performance, using your original figures as a benchmark.

APPLYING THE FINDINGS

The assessor's feedback therefore should include:

- issues on which action is required over the three year period
- a reminder to employers that IIP involves continuous development
- encouragement to the organisation to retain its existing portfolio, and to add to the portfolio when existing systems are changed or new ones are added to adjust to changes in staff deployment, production or services provided.

During the three year period, in any dynamic organisation, many changes will occur. Not all of the results of these will be totally obvious, *eg* the need for equivalent training and development.

Re-recognition, of course, will be against the Standard as before. It is not a requirement that the business concerned will have to produce better results and better evidence than before. It should continue to be 'naturally occurring' in the form of documents on change, memos, minutes and certificates.

The assessment indicators should remain consistent. Neither is it required that the reassessment should involve the same assessor or assessors, but it might be more economical since previous experience of the organisation would require less orientation.

Maintaining contact

To help the process of continuing improvement, it is recommended that TECs/LECs maintain contact on a yearly basis with recognised organisations and that application for re-recognition should be submitted six months before the due date. It would therefore be advantageous to keep the same working group to respond to changes, to organise processes and to collect evidence.

IMPROVING DOCUMENTATION

It is not absolutely essential to retain all of the original portfolio. The assessor, however, has to look for contemporary and valid evidence. For those parts of the portfolio which remain totally relevant to the present, it would be sensible to keep them, whilst also collecting new evidence for changes. If in the course of the three years the business has added new dimensions, or has been subject to a takeover, there may well be big changes in organisation, management, production and business strategies. All of these will have to be included within the revised portfolio.

REFINING AND IMPROVING

The effect of changes on business related training and development could also be investigated by means of re-runs of employee surveys. Standard questionnaires or diagnostic questionnaires, such as those described earlier in this book, or relevant questions of your own, could be applied to ascertain employee opinions on training required, especially in new processes, and evaluations of previous or contemporary training (see Figure 12). Investors in People is essentially about continuous improvement.

Identifying new evidence

Another approach to re-recognition which would enable you to identify your present position on evidence is to take each of the indicators and ask four specific questions (*Guide to self review*, IIP Scotland):

Training you have received during the past year				
Title	*VQ or other qualification*	*Tutor(s)*	*Rating A,B,C,D,E*	*Comments: relevance/quality*

How would you rate your present performance?
Place a tick in the box which applies to you:

Do not have any of the essential competences ❑

Do not have some of the competences ❑

Have all the necessary competences ❑

Have more than the necessary competences ❑

Describe the competences you lack:

Signed:

Fig. 12. Examples of questionnaire items evaluating recent training.

1. What modifications have been made?

2. Why did you make the modifications?

3. What documentation exists to demonstrate this?

4. What benefits have you identified as a result?

5. (Complete this question only if the answer to Question 1 is None.) What documents will demonstrate that the unchanged practices are still applied effectively?

See Figure 13 for sample answers.

Example of self review of one indicator
2.3 A process exists for regularly reviewing the training and development needs of all employees. 1. *What modifications have you made?* We have added our own survey questionnaire of employees' views on training needs and development and on evaluations of recent training. 2. *Why did you make the modifications?* The new information might support the views of management or point to other conclusions. Evaluations by those who have experienced training are often more valid than those of observers of effects. 3. *What documentation exists to demonstrate this?* The new questionnaire and summary of the information recently provided by it. 4. *What benefits have you identified as a result?* Modifications to previous managerial views, leading to actions causing improved production and profit.

Fig. 13. Method for identifying new training needs prior to reassessment.

Sequencing the re-recognition process

The process of re-recognition therefore requires:

- analytic examination/scrutiny of the written evidence provided (portfolio)
- the interviewing of a sample of employees to confirm that existing and new practices are functioning effectively
- evidence of continuing business improvement parallel to IIP
- a report by the assessor to the Recognition Panel

- a decision by the panel
- a feedback meeting between members of the organisation with representatives of LEC/TEC, etc, and the assessor.

Some organisations may ask: 'Why go through all this again? Why be reassessed?' The following extract may help to answer their questions.

> Many of the metaphors used about IIP portray it as a journey with a destination where the goal is recognition. This is an inevitable side-effect of league tables and targets, but I think it is flawed.
>
> Take the parcels firm TNT, for example, which was widely quoted during last month's IIP week. 'The main reason for undertaking the whole process was that we saw it as part of our journey towards achieving total quality within the business', TNT's personnel director, David Hanley, said in the September issue of *Training and Enterprise Journal*. If IIP is part of a journey, is it then a landmark you aim for, reach and then leave behind? Or is it better thought of as a 10,000 mile service – a periodic chance to benchmark your firm's approach to training against external standard? That's how Dorset TEC sees it. Its chief executive, John Morrison, says, 'As the TEC and its Investors move forward, we will be sharing best practice networking and helping each other create an environment of leading-edge development companies in Dorset'.
>
> As the scheme matures and more companies come around for a second time, we need to take a leaf out of Dorset TEC's book and place more emphasis on the continuous improvement aspect.
>
> Ian Mackinnon, Consultant, Segal, Quince Wicksteed. *People Management*, 19 October 1995.

Finally – any quality programme can only function properly in the right kind of environment. So if you are enthusiastic about Investors in People – remember to keep to all the requirements of Health and Safety Regulations.

VISIBLE RECOGNITION

Having achieved Investors in People, you are now entitled to:

- use the logo on all your documentation
- display the metallic badge at your premises
- fly an IIP flag.

SUMMARY

- The assessor's feedback.
- Identifying improvements to be made in the evidence.
- Presenting findings to the Recognition Panel.
- Qualifications of assessors.
- The role of the panel.
- Preparing for re-recognition.
- Applying the findings of the first assessment.
- Improving the portfolio and interview evidence.
- Refining and improving IIP systems.
- New evidence, *eg* questionnaires.
- Why be reassessed?

CASE STUDY

Alex makes her point

'I'm sure you all thought I was mad when I suggested at one of our discussions a year or two ago that we should go for IIP immediately after ISO9000.'

'Oh no, Alex', protested Mary Hughes, 'we knew you were right but we did wonder if we had the time to do it.'

'Time, time!' expostulated Alex. 'As I often say if you have real enthusiasm and motivation, time doesn't matter – you get caught up in it.'

No one in the meeting felt that argument on this occasion was on the cards. They knew that they had had to make a big effort, with occasional signs of stress, but that in the end all had gone well.

'Well, we did succeed', said Alex with a satisfied smile. 'Now we have to look ahead three years to reassessment. I've just been looking at a report in *People Management.* I quote:

> Firms that sign up to the Investors in People Standard are more likely to empower their staff, according to a report published at the (IPD) conference.
>
> The study, conducted by Cranfield and the Host Consultancy for Investors in People (UK), said those companies which have attained IIP status enjoy more effective planning and goal setting, improved staff motivation and better internal communications as a result.
>
> IIP companies are also more productive and more profitable, according to the Report. Strangely, however, the research found that non-IIP companies were more likely to give line managers responsibility for HR-related issues.
>
> 'IIP does not have a monopoly of good practice,' admitted Jane Drown, Development Manager at IIP (UK).

'Now', observed Alex, 'we have vastly increased business along with achieving IIP, but I think of our meetings and indeed our culture as being democratic and that you all have independent responsibility. So we happen to be getting the best of all the worlds.'

'I'm certainly not going to get caught up in which is the better approach, employee or task centred management', thought Mary, who was now on an MBA course, 'but we certainly did achieve IIP – maybe we were just good at our jobs and IIP helped to make us better.'

'Wake up, Mary', shouted Alex, 'you're not listening to me. As one of my top line managers I want you to start immediately on preparation for re-recognition in 1999. You know that the assessor told us we were not quite so effective in evaluation as we might be – please start on this now, benchmarking against our last two years' performance. Remember, we are looking for continuous improvement.'

Question

It appears that Alex Thomson-Bell, an authoritarian manager, is beginning to see that Investors in People is more than just a kind of status symbol – that it does bring about business improvements. Do you think that IIP also improves quality of management – if so, how does this happen?

DISCUSSION POINTS

1. Is there a risk that an organisation which achieves IIP will tend to rest on its laurels and do very little before the re-recognition process? Would this mean they would not ask to be reassessed?
2. Do you think that three years is about the right amount of time before reassessment? Should the timescale be longer or shorter? Justify your views.

3. Great care is taken to ensure that no one on the Recognition Panel would be biased in any way in helping it to reach a decision. What kinds of views might there be for deciding that a panel member could not take part in consideration of a particular organisation?

4. Do you agree that the need to be reassessed by organisations depends very largely on the continuing status and desirability of re-recognition as well as on the practical effects on your own business? If so, why are these factors regarded as so important?

Appendix
Investors in People: The Four Principles and Indicators

The four principles of the Investors in People National Standard have been broken down into 24 indicators which are the basis for assessment.

1 COMMITMENT

An Investor in People makes a public commitment from the top to develop all employees to achieve its business objectives.

- Every employer should have a written but flexible plan which sets out business goals and targets, considers how employees will contribute to achieving the plan and specifies how development needs in particular will be assessed and met.

- Management should develop and communicate to all employees a vision of where the organisation is going and the contribution employees will make to its success, involving employee representatives as appropriate.

Assessment indicators

1.1 There is a public commitment from the most senior level within the organisation to develop people.

1.2 Employees at all levels are aware of the broad aims or vision of the organisation.

1.3 There is a written but flexible plan which sets out business goals and targets.

1.4 The plan identifies broad development needs and specifies how they will be assessed and met.

1.5 The employer has considered what employees at all levels will contribute to the success of the organisation and has communicated this effectively to them.

1.6 Where representative structures exist, management communicates with employee representatives a vision of where the organisation is going and the contribution employees (and their representatives) will make to its success.

2 PLANNING

An Investor in People regularly reviews the needs and plans the training and development of all employees.

- The resources for training and developing employees should be clearly identified in the business plan.
- Managers should be responsible for regularly agreeing training and development needs with each employee in the context of business objectives, setting targets and standards linked, where appropriate to the achievement of National Vocational Qualifications (or relevant units) and in Scotland, Scottish Vocational Qualifications.

Assessment indicators

2.1 The written plan identifies the resources that will be used to meet training and development needs.

2.2 Training and development needs are regularly reviewed against business objectives.

2.3 A process exists for regularly reviewing the training and development needs of all employees.

2.4 Responsibility for developing people is clearly identified throughout the organisation, starting at the top.

2.5 Managers are competent to carry our their responsibilities for developing people.

2.6 Targets and standards are set for development actions.

2.7 Where appropriate, training targets are linked to achieving external standards, and particularly to National Vocational Qualifications (or Scottish Vocational Qualifications in Scotland) and units.

3 ACTION

An Investor in People takes action to train and develop individuals on recruitment and throughout their employment.

- Action should focus on the training needs of all new recruits and continually developing and improving the skills of existing employees.
- All employees should be encouraged to contribute to identifying and meeting their own job-related development needs.

Assessment indicators

3.1 All new employees are introduced effectively to the organisation and are given the training and development they need to do their jobs.

3.2 The skills of existing employees are developed in line with business objectives.

3.3 All employees are made aware of the development opportunities open to them.

3.4 All employees are encouraged to help identify and meet their job-related development needs.

3.5 Effective action takes place to achieve the training and development objectives of individuals and the organisation.

3.6 Managers are actively involved in supporting employees to meet their training and development needs.

4 EVALUATION

An Investor in People evaluates the investment in training and development to assess achievement and improve future effectiveness.

- The investment, the competence and commitment of employees, and the use made of skills learned should be reviewed at all levels against business goals and targets.
- The effectiveness of training and development should be reviewed at the top level and lead to renewed commitment and target setting.

Assessment indicators

4.1 The organisation evaluates how its development of people is contributing to business goals and targets.

4.2 The organisation evaluates whether its development actions have achieved their objectives.

4.3 The outcomes of training and development are evaluated at individual, team and organisational levels.

4.4 Top management understand the broad costs and benefits of developing people.

4.5 The continuing commitment of top management to developing people is communicated to all employees.

There will be wide differences in the approach to training and development, depending on the size of each organisation, structure, markets and business objectives. All will affect the way in which an organisation seeks to meet the Standard – the assessment process respects these differences.

Glossary

Annual report. The means by which an organisation can inform the shareholders, interested parties or the public in general of its activities and progress, including basic financial information, over the previous year.

Appraisal. A process, usually an interview, where line manager (appraiser) and employee (appraisee) can review the latter's progress on the job since the previous appraisal, identify new training needs and decide how these should be met. Some appraisals also consider future pay levels or possible promotion.

Assessor. The person who, by studying evidence obtained from written documentation and verbal sources, decides whether to recommend to a Recognition Panel that the organisation concerned has at this stage reached the National Standard or not and what may still be left to do. His/her work is monitored by an internal verifier.

Attitude. A relatively stable disposition towards a person, group or social issue.

Benchmarking. Comparing an organisation's performance in detail with that of its business competitors.

Board of directors. A group of officials who determine the general strategy of an organisation.

Briefing. Detailed orders or informal session with groups starting a new activity or course of action.

BS5750. See 'Quality'.

Business plan. A written strategy to guide an organisation over a specific period of time, including its objectives, how they will be reached and the training required by employees.

Chief executive. The official in everyday charge of an organisation and who implements the policies of the board of directors.

Citizens Charter. A government quality initiative, signified by a Charter Mark, especially for public services, verifying a group's contention that it is upholding its own excellent standards.

Commitment. Binding oneself or an organisation to a principle or course of action.

Communication. The transmission of spoken, written and pictorial symbols between people to convey and facilitate meaning.

Competence. A specific skill required to perform a job effectively. Most jobs require a number of interlinked competences.

Consultant. An expert, usually in a specific field, who is hired by an organisation to help it to improve in that particular area. Sometimes clients do not know how best to use or apply this expertise.

Counselling interview. A two-way discussion process between a counsellor and client in which the former, by encouraging the client to talk about his/her concerns (either general issues or a career requirement), clarifies the issues for the client and helps enable him/her to decide on appropriate action.

Cultural change. An alteration, sometimes, radical in the *modus operandi* of an organisation – affecting every aspect and often extremely difficult to implement because of in-built habit.

Development. The process of acquiring new skills, knowledge and competences often built on existing ones, either deliberately and sequentially through one's organisation or sometimes as the result of general experience.

Development interview. Similar to the appraisal interview, this is a constructive consideration of an employee's learning needs as part of continuing career development within an organisation.

Diagnostic assessment. A systematically constructed questionnaire which, when completed by staff members, helps to identify processes (such as in Investors in People) still required to be put in place.

Distance learning. Learning in which the instructional and informational source is physically separated from the learner and where communication is via postal services, telephone, computer programme, television or E mail.

Empower. Employees are given a say in how their jobs are done, *eg* teams are delegated more authority and ownership of a project, encouraging greater initiative and thereby increased motivation.

Equal opportunities. A policy sometimes supported by legislation (*eg* sex, race, disability) in which discrimination is disallowed. Equal opportunities in training and development would certainly be expected of Investors in People employers as they must show that they develop **all** employees if necessary to reach business targets.

Evaluate. To place a value on or estimate of the worth of a process, *eg* a training programme.

Feedback loop. A continuing process in which the production results of the work of an individual or group are communicated to management, who may make some changes. Further feedback can show whether the changes have produced improvement. Quick knowledge of good results can be very motivating to production workers.

Flexibility. The ability of an individual, team or organisation to respond rapidly to changing requirements.

Focus group/Network. A group of organisations, linked by a common project (*eg* Investors in People), who meet together to further the project, partly through mutual help.

Goals/Targets. Specific objectives which should be set for individuals, teams and organisations (sometimes through benchmarking) as part of a business plan.

Hierarchy of needs. A theory of needs by Abraham Maslow suggesting that all individuals are motivated by the same sequence of needs which are arranged in levels of importance, *ie* once 'lower' needs are largely satisfied, then an individual is motivated by those further up the hierarchy, *eg* needs for safety are at a lower level than self-esteem which, in turn, is lower than self-actualisation.

Human resource development (HRD). Department or group within an organisation which specialises in or co-ordinates the training and development of employees.

Induction programme. A series of planned experiences which enable a new employee or an employee who has changed department to adjust more rapidly to new conditions. It involves being made aware of his/her role within the whole range of the company products or services as well as within a specific team.

IPD (Institute of Personnel and Development). Professional organisation consisting mainly of specialists in human resource development, personnel and training.

In-tray exercises. A technique, usually involved in selecting managerial staff, in which applicants have to show how they would deal with practical/everyday situations and problems within the organisation.

Intrinsic satisfaction. Being motivated by feelings of interest and competence within the job rather than by extrinsic factors, *eg* money.

ISO9000. See 'Quality'.

Investors in People. A quality programme in which the central issue is that employee training and development during their working lifetime should be systematically directed towards achieving the objectives of the organisation's business plan for growth and company development.

Job description. A written set of the details of all the activities, competences, skills and responsibilities involved in a specific job. The description is important in appraising an employee and agreeing on training and development needs.

Leadership qualities. The characteristics required to ensure that every employee gives of their best as part of a common purpose towards business success which may involve constant change.

Learning organisation. An organisation (a complex arrangement of linked groups) where change is the norm, where training and development is integral and where learning is directed towards increased productivity, quality and customer satisfaction.

Line manager. An individual at a particular position in a hierarchical management structure. Increasingly appraisals are carried out by line managers, who have been properly trained to do so, for those they supervise.

Local Enterprise Company. The Scottish LECs have the same function in Scotland as the TECs have in England and the Training and Employment Agency in Northern Ireland. Additionally they have economic development and environmental improvement functions.

Management Charter Initiative. Part of the NCVQ concept, it acts as the lead body for management standards. These standards are formulated very similarly to VQs. The MCI works with TECs, LECs and Chambers of Commerce to provide support and awareness locally for managerial development.

Matrix system. A diagrammatic method for ascertaining whether sufficient evidence is matched against the assessment indicators of the Investors in People Standard.

Mentor. An experienced, reliable person within an organisation who acts as a 'model' and adviser to less experienced and probably younger employees.

Mission statement. Summarises for an organisation its vision and defines the essential purpose for each person in their particular roles.

Motivation. The ways in which individual or group behaviour is energised, directed and sustained.

Multiple sites. The same organisation may operate from different offices or factories over the whole of the UK. They may all produce the same goods or perform the same functions or they could be totally different.

Multi-skill. A term used to describe the idea that an employee can have several different skills, as opposed to a totally specialised one, and that qualifications across skills should be developed.

National Vocational Qualification/Scottish Vocational Qualification. Workplace assessed qualifications accredited by the NCVQ, National Council for Vocational Qualifications working through established examining and awarding bodies (*eg* City and Guilds, BTEC, RSA, LCCIEB). The Scottish equivalents are SVQs, qualifications defined by lead bodies just as with NVQs. SCOTVEC (The Scottish Vocational Education Council) also has responsibility for developing, awarding and accrediting these qualifications.

Negotiate. To settle a dispute or argument by discussion, by trying to reach agreement, through bargaining or arriving at a compromise solution.

Objectives. See goals.

Performance indicator. A written statement pointing to the actions an organisation must take (in Investors in People) to reach the level required by this part of the Standard.

Personal development plan. Can be either an individual's training and development plan relating to his/her job or a 'personal' one in the sense that it is specific to that person's needs.

Pilot study. An experimental trial of a new approach or technique to ascertain if it works or needs modifications before being fully implemented.

Portfolio. A collection of paper and other evidence (*eg* videos) which helps an assessor (Investors in People) to decide if the Standard has been reached.

Primary evidence. This is portfolio evidence (see above).

Profit. The amount by which the revenue of a company exceeds its costs (one criterion indicating improved performance).

Psychometric test. A standardised test of ability, personality, attainment, aptitude or interest which should be valid and reliable and have norms which enable an organisation to assess an individual in a selection or training needs situation.

Quality. Represents a high standard of service or production. Total Quality Management (TQM) relates to ensuring that a push towards high standards in these processes occurs at all stages. ISO9000, formerly BS5750, helps ensure that adherence to pre-determined quality levels is maintained during the production process. The Citizens Charter relates to quality in the public services signified by the Charter Mark. Investors in People ensures the quality of the training and development of staff in working towards the targets of the business plan.

Recognition panel. A group of suitably qualified people recruited by recognition units and mainly from a business background, whose responsibility is to weigh-up the evidence and the report of the assessor to decide whether an organisation should be recognised as an Investor in People.

Recognition units. Manage the assessment process within a particular area. Provide a recognition service via TECs, the Training and Enterprise Agency in Northern Ireland, Investors in People, Scotland, and Investors in People UK. Must prove to external verifier from IIP (UK) that they meet the agreed quality assurance criteria.

Reinforcement (of behaviour). Any behaviour which is positively reinforced (by praise, reward or a wished-for result) tends to be repeated.

Re-recognition. An organisation which has achieved the IIP Standard can apply to be re-recognised after a three year period.

Resources. People, facilities and materials which enable an organisation to reach its objectives.

Review. A wide-ranging consideration (in IIP) where the training needs of an individual or a whole organisation are under consideration.

Role. A function within a group or team, intended to make team work more efficient.

Scottish Enterprise. Has an executive and co-ordinating role in relation to local enterprise companies, including important aspects of the Investors in People strategy. There is an equivalent Highlands and Islands Enterprise.

Scottish Vocational Qualification. See National Vocational Qualification.

Secondary evidence. Evidence from interview sources (for IIP).

Self-esteem. Thinking well of oneself. A manager or employee will have increased self-esteem if they feel they have contributed to company success by completing a training programme successfully.

Senior management. The top echelon of management, including the chief executive and heads of large divisions or departments.

Simulation. An assessment situation (for VQs) where it is not possible to assess an individual in a 'real' situation so it is simulated to be as near to reality as possible.

Standard. A criterion laid down by an authorised body which, in their considered opinion, acts as a model for the level of efficiency required.

Survey questionnaire. A series of questions relevant to an organisation's need for awareness of the views of its staff on a specific question, *eg* their training and development needs.

Team. A group of employees who co-operate with each other so as to reach a common aim or goal.

Team role. See Role. M Belbin suggests such roles as chairperson, 'plant' (creative thinker), completer/finisher, monitor/evaluator.

Training. The process of acquiring skills, underpinning knowledge and qualifications through teaching and instruction in the workplace or by following an external course so as to improve performance.

Training and Employment Agency. Similar role to TECs and LECs in Northern Ireland.

Training and Enterprise Councils. The network of independent companies in England and Wales, run by boards of directors, mainly from the private sector, but publicly funded, whose functions are to develop training in local businesses, encourage enterprise (small business start ups), provide training for the unemployed and promote Investors in People and Business Links programmes. The TEC National Council develops policy and facilitates communication.

Training budget. An amount of money set aside and 'ring fenced' for paying the costs of training and developing employees. An important factor in IIP.

Training needs analysis. Ascertaining training needs of employees by means of a comprehensive survey or detailed interview programme. Information could be categorised into general organisational training needs. An analysis would be restricted to a smaller group within the whole organisation.

Training record. A list of all the training experienced over a certain period by individuals or team or both.

Turnover. The amount of money representing the total price of all the goods and services sold by an organisation within a fixed time.

Vision. A far reaching view of the future prospects of an organisation, summed up as effectively as possible by a mission statement, *eg* Henry Ford producing 'cars for all'.

Working group. An ad hoc group of employees, given a particular task, usually cross-departmental, *eg* Investors in People group.

Further Reading

American Psychologist Special Issue: Organizational Psychology, Volume 45 No. 2, February 1990

Effective Managerial Communication, R. W. Rasberry & F. F. Lemoine (Kent Publishing Company, 1986)

Frontiers of Excellence. Learning from Companies that Put People First, Robert Waterman (Nicholas Brealey Publishing, 1995)

Implementing NVQ's, Edward Fennell (Compendium No. 3 Employment Department Group, 1994)

Investors in People and Management Standards. Management Charter Initiative, 1993

Investors in People Standard, IIP 80, 1995. *How to Become an Investor in People*, IIP 82, 1995. *Towards World Class Performance – Investors in People and Quality Standards*, IIP 89. Available from Investors in People UK, PO Box 204, London SE99 7UW.

Investors in People Scotland Main publications, *Diagnostic Pack Development Workbook, Assessment Framework, Guide to Self Review* (Available from LECs)

Investors in People: What's It To Do with NVQ's, Edward Fennell (Competence and Assessment Issue 19 Employment Department Group, 1992)

Management and Organisational Behaviour, Laurie J., Mullins (Pictorial Publishing 3rd Edition, 1993)

Managing for Success. Improving Business Performance through Employee Involvement No. 2. Motivating for Performance (CBI and Employment Department Group, July 1991)

Managing People at Work, Peter Makin, Cary Cooper, Charles Cox (British Psychological Society and Routledge Ltd, 1989)

Measure Up! R. L. Lynch & K. F. Cross (Mandarin, 1991)

Towards a Career Resilient Workforce, R. H. Waterman, Jr, Judith A, Waterman & Betsy A. Collard (Harvard Business Review July–August, 1994)

Training and Development: Communique, Mary Chapman (Vol. 12 No. 11 November 1994)

Why Employers Need Occupational Standards, NVQ's and SVQ's, Graham Debling (Competence and Assessment Compendium No. 3 Employment Department Group, 1994)

Work Psychology. Understanding Human Behaviour in the Workplace, J. Arnold, I. T. Robertson and C. L. Cooper (Longman Group U.K. Ltd, 1991)

Useful Addresses

If you are interested in Investors in People, telephone your local TEC or LEC, your first point of contact.

Advisory Scottish Council for Education and Training Targets (ASCETT), Professor John M. Ward, IBM (UK) Ltd, 120 Bothwell Street, Glasgow G2 7JP. Tel: (0141) 228 2532. Fax: (0141) 228 2449.

British Psychological Society, 48 Princess Road East, Leicester LE1 7DR. Tel: (0116) 254 9568. Fax: (0116) 247 0787. For information on Certificates in Competence (Levels A and B) in Occupational Testing.

Business and Technology Education Council, Central House, Upper Woburn Place, London WCD1H 0HH. Tel: (0171) 413 8400. Fax: (0171) 387 6068.

City and Guilds, Customer Services Enquiry Unit, 1 Giltspur Street, London EC1A 9DD. Tel: (0171) 294 2468. Fax: (0171) 294 2400.

Department for Education and Employment (DfEE), Moorfoot, Sheffield S1 4PQ. Tel: (0114) 275 3275.

Equal Opportunities Commission, Overseas House, Quay Street, Manchester M3 3HN. Tel: (0161) 833 9244.

Highland and Islands Enterprise, Bridge House, 20 Bridge Street, Inverness IV1 1QR. Tel: (01463) 234 171. Fax: (01463) 244 469.

Institute of Personnel and Development, IPD House, Camp Road, London SW19 4UX. Tel: (0181) 971 9000. Fax: (0181) 263 3333.

Investors in People Scotland, 1 Washington Court, Washington Lane, Edinburgh EH11 2HA. Tel: (0131) 346 1212. Fax: (0131) 346 2525.

Investors in People UK, Chief Executive, 7-10 Chandos Street, London W1M 9DE. Tel: (0171) 467 1900. Fax: (0171) 636 2386.

London Chamber of Commerce and Industry Examination Board, Marlowe House, Station Road, Sidcup, Kent DA15 7BJ. Tel: (0181) 392 0261. Fax: (0181) 302 4169.

The Management Charter Initiative, Russell Square House, 10–12 Russell Square, London WC1B 5BZ. Tel: (0171) 872 9000. Fax: (0171) 872 9099.

National Advisory Council for Education and Training Targets (NACETT), 222 Gray's Inn Road, London WC1X 8HL.

National Council for Vocational Qualifications, 222 Euston Road, London NW1 2BZ. Tel: (0171) 387 9898. Fax: (0171) 387 0978.

National Council of Industry Training Organisations, Unit 10, Meadowcourt, 10 Amos Road, Sheffield S9 1OX. Tel: (0114) 261 9926. Fax: (0114) 261 8103.

RSA Examinations Board, Westwood Way, Coventry CV4 8HS. Tel: (01203) 470033. Fax: (01203) 468080.

Scottish Enterprise, 120 Bothwell Street, Glasgow G2 7JP. Tel: (0141) 248 2700. Fax: (0141) 221 3217.

Scottish Vocational Education Council (SCOTVEC), Hanover House, 24 Douglas Street, Glasgow G2 7NQ. Tel: (0141) 248 7900. Fax: (0141) 242 2244.

TEC National Council, 10th Floor, Westminster Tower, 3 Albert Embankment, London SE1 7SP. Tel: (0171) 735 0010.

Training and Development Lead Body, c/o Employment Occupational Standards Council, 2 Savoy Court, The Strand, London WC2R 0EZ. Tel: (0171) 240 6264. Fax: (0171) 240 6264.

Training and Employment Agency, Clarendon House, 9/21 Adelaide Street, Belfast, Northern Ireland BT2 8NR. Tel: (01232) 541 541. Fax: (01232) 541 542.

The Training and Enterprise Directory, Kogan Page Limited, 120 Pentonville Road, London N1 9JN.

Index

HOW TO CONDUCT STAFF APPRAISALS
A practical handbook for every manager today

Nigel Hunt

Managers and organisations neglect staff appraisal at their peril today. But what exactly is staff appraisal? Is it something to be welcomed or feared? Why is it now so vital, and what are the benefits? Should senior as well as junior staff undergo appraisal, and how could this be done? Which managers should do the appraisals, and how should they start? This book, now in a new edition, sets out a basic framework which every manager can use or adapt, whether in business and industry, transport, education, health and public services. Nigel Hunt is a consultant in occupational testing, selection, appraisal, vocational assessment, and management development. He is a Graduate Member of the British Psychological Society, and Associate Member of the Institute of Personnel & Development. 'Informative . . . Points for discussion and case studies are prominent throughout . . . the case studies are highly relevant and good.' *Progress (NEBS Management Association Journal).* 'Not all books live up to their promises. This one does. At the price it is a bargain.' *British Journal of Administrative Management.*

154pp. illus. 1 85703 117 2. 2nd edition.

ORGANISING EFFECTIVE TRAINING
How to plan and run successful courses and seminars

James Chalmers

Industry, public services, colleges, community groups, and organisations of all kinds urgently need to train their people in a wide variety of much needed skills. But however knowledgeable the tutors are, if a training event has been badly organised it will be a waste of everyone's time and money. This book explains how to plan and organise really successful training events. The method can be applied to anything, from team building to technical courses, and from a one hour briefing up to events lasting several days. The step-by-step approach is easy to follow, and will work equally well with organisers who are unfamiliar with the subject to be trained, as well as professional trainers. If you are ever asked to put on an event, or if you want someone to run one for you, then this will give all the necessary guidance and ensure a successful outcome every time. James Chalmers

BSc CEng MIEE has worked in industry for 25 years, and has much experience of running successful training programmes.

160pp. illus. 1 85703 329 9.

HOW TO MANAGE AN OFFICE
Creating and managing a successful workplace

Ann Dobson

Good office management is one of the keys to success in any organisation. The benefits are a happy and productive staff, satisfied customers, and a sound base from which to tackle such issues as growth and change within the organisation. Written by an experienced office manager and business consultant, this book suggests a complete practical framework for the well run office. It discusses what an office is for, the office as communications, the office as workplace, equipment, hygiene, health and security, external appearances, managing visitors, handling orders and information, managing office supplies, the office budget, staff management, and managing an office move.

160 pp. illus. 1 85703 049 4.

TAKING ON STAFF
How to recruit the right people into your organisation

David Greenwood

In any organisation three things are sure: people are the key to winning the competitive edge; when a company needs to recruit it's in a hurry; and few things can be as disastrous as a bad recruitment decision. *Taking on Staff* is designed for the manager in a hurry. It is a practical off-the-peg recruitment and selection package suitable for every kind of organisation and job. It covers the whole process from defining the organisation's needs, and ending with the induction of new staff. At every stage it explains how to collect, evaluate and record evidence about a candidate's potential to meet their organisation's needs. The book is complete with checklists, specimen forms, contracts, letters and typical case studies. David Greenwood is Personnel Officer for the Government of the Island of Jersey, and an NVQ Assessor.

160 pp. illus. 1 85703 189 X.

HOW TO COUNSEL PEOPLE AT WORK
A practical approach to staff care

John Humphries

The value of counselling has become much better recognised in recent times, as a tool for addressing a whole variety of human situations. This new book has been specially written for everyone wanting to know how to make use of counselling techniques in the workplace. It discusses what is counselling, the role of the counsellor, communication skills, body language/verbal behaviour, styles of counselling, managing counselling interviews, and the uses of counselling. The book is complete with helpful checklists, case studies, self-assessment material and points for discussion, key addresses, glossary and index.

104 pp. illus. 1 85703 093 1.

HOW TO MANAGE PEOPLE AT WORK
A practical guide to effective leadership

John Humphries

'These days, if a textbook on people management is to succeed, it must be highly informative, reliable, comprehensive – and eminently user-friendly. Without doubt, *How to Manage People at Work* is one such book. Written in an attractive style that should appeal to any first-line manager who has neither the time nor the energy to cope with heavy reading, John Humphries has tackled this extremely wide subject ably and well. Rightly or wrongly, it has always been my experience that one has only to read the first couple of pages of any textbook on people management to discover whether or not the author enjoys an empathy with the people at the sharp end – and here is one author who, for my money, has passed the test with flying colours.' *Progress/NEBS Management Association.*

160 pp. illus. 1 85703 068 0. 2nd edition.

CONDUCTING EFFECTIVE INTERVIEWS
How to prepare and how to achieve the right outcomes

Ann Dobson

At one time only senior management would carry out interviews.

Nowadays, however, effective delegation in large organisations, coupled with the number of small businesses being set up, means that more and more working people at all levels are becoming involved in interviewing. Whether you are interviewing a job applicant, dealing with disciplinary procedures or organising a decision-making session, this new book will provide you with all the information you need to achieve your aims. Part 1 offers a step-by-step guide to the general principles of interviewing and Part 2 illustrates the various types of interviews you may be involved with in your working life. Case studies are used to show how the same interview can be dealt with in a successful or unsuccessful way. Ann Dobson is Principal of a Secretarial Training School, and has had long professional experience of interview techniques in theory and practice.

160 pp. illus. 1 85703 223 3.

MANAGING MEETINGS
How to prepare, how to take part and how to follow up

Ann Dobson

Meetings can be interesting, productive and even fun! That is the message this new 'How To' book seeks to convey. Meetings form a large part of our lives today, particularly in the business world, yet many of us feel ill equipped to handle them with ease. The book is divided into two parts: the first covers the key skills of communicating effectively, motivating and persuading, problem solving, decision making, body language, and dealing with troublemakers. Part 2 deals with the practical steps of holding a meeting and following up. Case studies, self-assessment material and checklists complete the simple, yet effective approach. Ann Dobson is Principal of a Secretarial Training School, and has been involved with meetings of varying types for many years. She is also the author of *How to Communicate at Work*, *How to Write Business Letters*, *How to Return to Work* and *How to Manage an Office* in this series.

128 pp. illus. 1 85703 222 5.

MANAGING YOURSELF
How to achieve your personal goals in life and at work

Julie-Ann Amos

Managing yourself is often more difficult than it seems. So many other people, events and things seem to take control of, exert influence over, or just interfere with our lives and how we want to behave. This simple book goes beyond assertiveness and behaviour, and examines how to deal *inside* ourselves with the daily conflicts of everyday life. The reader will learn how to handle criticism, thoughts and emotions, aggression, passivity, change, conflict, and stress, through developing assertive communications and listening skills, body language and confidence. Julie-Ann Amos is a Member of the Institute of Personnel and Development. She is a Senior Personnel Officer and Trainer with a large local authority, and has taught Assertiveness and Personal Effectiveness programmes for many years. She has post-graduate qualifications in both Personnel and Administrative Management.

160 pp. illus. 1 85703 324 8.

STARTING TO MANAGE
How to prepare yourself for a more responsible role at work

Julie-Ann Amos

Management is not in itself difficult. The problem is, it isn't always easy, either. This practical introduction gives a broad overview of management, to dispel much of the mystery which surrounds it. It is intended for all new managers, supervisors, students and anyone who hopes to enter management. It explains the various basic theories surrounding management, and put these into a practical everyday context. The reader will learn how to manage workloads, decisions, stock, equipment, money, legislation, customers, staff, and much more besides. The book will make an ideal launch pad for everyone wanting to start taking responsibility and influence events in their own organisation. Julie-Ann Amos BSc is a graduate of the Universities of East Anglia and Portsmouth, and Member of the Institute of Personnel and Development. She is a Senior Personnel Officer and trainer with a large local authority, and has post-graduate qualifications in both Personnel and Administrative Management.

160 pp. illus. 1 85703 319 1.

HOW TO COMMUNICATE AT WORK
Making a success of your working relationships

Ann Dobson

Things only get done properly at work if everyone communicates effectively – whatever their individual role in the organisation. This very practical step-by-step guide gets to the very basics of good communication – what it is and why we need it, how to speak and listen, how to ask and answer questions, how to take messages and use the telephone; how to liaise, negotiate, persuade, offer advice and accept criticism; how to stand up for yourself, dealing with shyness, a difficult boss or angry customer; how to use and understand body language properly, how to cope with visitors, how to store and present information, how to use the English language correctly – and a great deal more, illustrated throughout with examples and case studies. Written by an experienced office staff trainer this book will be a real help to all young people starting a new job, or older individuals returning to work after time away.

192 pp. illus. 1 85703 103 2.

HOW TO MANAGE A SALES TEAM
A practical guide to sales leadership

John Humphries

However good an organisation's product or services, it still has to communicate those benefits to potential customers. The quality of a sales team can be crucial to the success or otherwise of an organisation, especially in the fiercely competitive marketplace of the 1990s. Written by a highly experienced training professional, this book meets the need for a practical handbook for every manager responsible for building or leading a sales team. With its useful checklists and case studies, it covers the whole subject from initial planning to recruitment, sales training, motivation and supervision, controlling budgets and forecasts, running sales meetings, and managing the sales function successfully within the organisation as a whole. John Humphries BSc has 18 years' professional experience as a management trainer. He is author of *How to Manage People at Work* in this series.

160 pp. illus. 1 85703 079 6.

How To Books

- ___ Selling into Japan (£14.99)
- ___ Setting up Home in Florida (£9.99)
- ___ Spend a Year Abroad (£8.99)
- ___ Start a Business from Home (£7.99)
- ___ Start a New Career (£6.99)
- ___ Starting to Manage (£8.99)
- ___ Starting to Write (£8.99)
- ___ Start Word Processing (£8.99)
- ___ Start Your Own Business (£8.99)
- ___ Study Abroad (£8.99)
- ___ Study & Learn (£7.99)
- ___ Study & Live in Britain (£7.99)
- ___ Studying at University (£8.99)
- ___ Studying for a Degree (£8.99)
- ___ Successful Grandparenting (£8.99)
- ___ Successful Mail Order Marketing (£9.99)
- ___ Successful Single Parenting (£8.99)
- ___ Survive at College (£4.99)
- ___ Survive Divorce (£8.99)
- ___ Surviving Redundancy (£8.99)
- ___ Take Care of Your Heart (£5.99)
- ___ Taking in Students (£8.99)
- ___ Taking on Staff (£8.99)
- ___ Taking Your A-Levels (£8.99)
- ___ Teach Abroad (£8.99)
- ___ Teach Adults (£8.99)
- ___ Teaching Someone to Drive (£8.99)
- ___ Travel Round the World (£8.99)
- ___ Use a Library (£6.99)
- ___ Use the Internet (£9.99)
- ___ Winning Consumer Competitions (£8.99)
- ___ Winning Presentations (£8.99)
- ___ Work from Home (£8.99)
- ___ Work in an Office (£7.99)
- ___ Work in Retail (£8.99)
- ___ Work with Dogs (£8.99)
- ___ Working Abroad (£14.99)
- ___ Working as a Holiday Rep (£9.99)
- ___ Working in Japan (£10.99)
- ___ Working in Photography (£8.99)
- ___ Working in the Gulf (£10.99)
- ___ Working on Contract Worldwide (£9.99)
- ___ Working on Cruise Ships (£9.99)
- ___ Write a CV that Works (£7.99)
- ___ Write a Press Release (£9.99)
- ___ Write a Report (£8.99)
- ___ Write an Assignment (£8.99)
- ___ Write an Essay (£7.99)
- ___ Write & Sell Computer Software (£9.99)
- ___ Write Business Letters (£8.99)
- ___ Write for Publication (£8.99)
- ___ Write for Television (£8.99)
- ___ Write Your Dissertation (£8.99)
- ___ Writing a Non Fiction Book (£8.99)
- ___ Writing & Selling a Novel (£8.99)
- ___ Writing & Selling Short Stories (£8.99)
- ___ Writing Reviews (£8.99)
- ___ Your Own Business in Europe (£12.99)

To: Plymbridge Distributors Ltd, Plymbridge House, Estover Road, Plymouth PL6 7PZ.
Customer Services Tel: (01752) 202301. Fax: (01752) 202331.

Please send me copies of the titles I have indicated. Please add postage & packing (UK £1, Europe including Eire, £2, World £3 airmail).

☐ I enclose cheque/PO payable to Plymbridge Distributors Ltd for £ ....

☐ Please charge to my ☐ MasterCard, ☐ Visa, ☐ AMEX card.

Account No. ☐☐☐☐☐☐☐☐☐☐☐☐☐☐☐☐

Card Expiry Date ☐☐ 19 ☐ ☎ **Credit Card orders may be faxed or phoned.**

Customer Name (CAPITALS) ....

Address ....

.... Postcode ....

Telephone .... Signature ....

Every effort will be made to despatch your copy as soon as possible but to avoid possible disappointment please allow up to 21 days for despatch time (42 days if overseas). Prices and availability are subject to change without notice.